From
the Library
of

No Witness

No Witness

Gerald A. Hausman

STACKPOLE BOOKS

Published by
STACKPOLE BOOKS
Cameron and Kelker Streets
P.O. Box 1831
Harrisburg, Pa. 17105

Published simultaneously in Don Mills, Ontario, Canada
by Thomas Nelson & Sons, Ltd.

Some of the names of persons and places contained in this book have been changed to protect their identity. Some of their characteristics have been exaggerated for artistic purposes. The events are factual but are not necessarily written in the exact sequence in which they occurred.

Maps by M. Balleydier
Jacket art by Craig Everhard

Printed in the U.S.A.

Library of Congress Cataloging in Publication Data

Hausman, Gerald.
  No witness.

  1. Animals, Treatment of—New Mexico.   2. Animals,
Treatment of—United States.   I. Title.
HV4765.N6H38 1980   636.08'3   80-23703
ISBN 0-8117-1009-2

For M.J.R.
with much appreciation

Contents

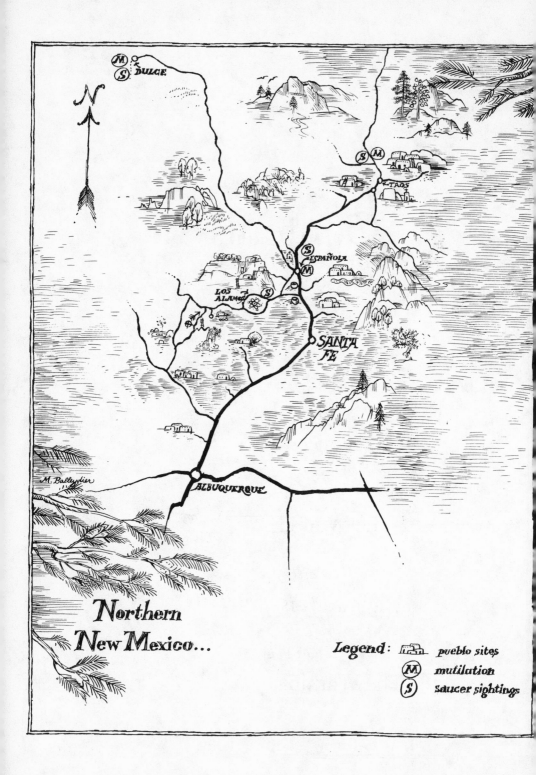

DULCE

TAOS

ESPAÑOLA

LOS
ALAMOS

SANTA
FE

ALBUQUERQUE

M. Ballydier

Northern
New Mexico...

Legend: pueblo sites

(M) mutilation

(S) saucer sightings

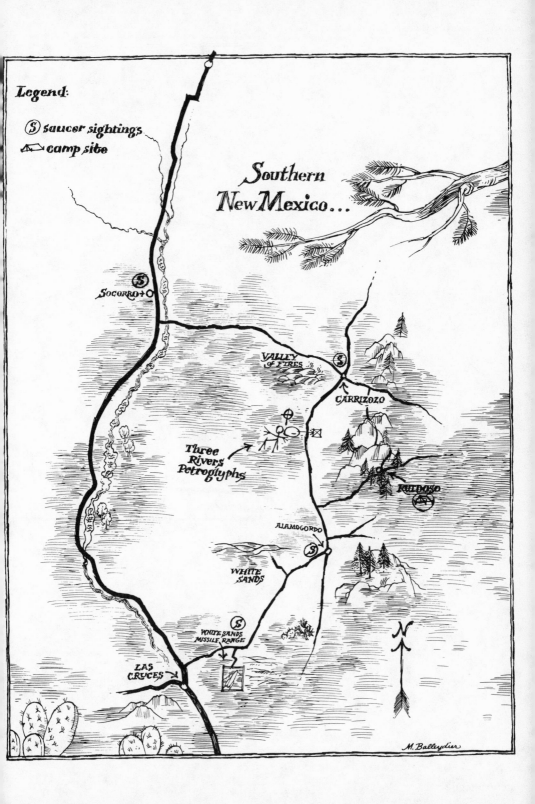

We arrived at dusk with four pails of garbage in the back of the pickup truck, my youngest daughter, Hannah, who is three, and myself. I don't like the dump at night, but we had a houseful of trash and company coming. I loaded up and came out with Hannah pulling at my sleeve because she likes to see the burrowing owls that feed on the mice and rats that prey upon the refuse.

The sun was down behind the Jemez Mountains when we got there and a night wind was on the plain. The dump was in a small hollow, the bare hills around it choked with paper. I emptied the cans quickly and called Hannah back from her owl watch. There was no answer. I scanned the landing strip where the owls had their headquarters, where you could see them at this hour readying their feathers for a low swoop and pick up of a mouse.

I called again for Hannah and saw nothing in the fast-coming darkness but papers rattling in the wind. A single burrowing owl took flight, flew off inches from the ground, its wingtips grazing the garbage. Now it was completely dark, but a thin hunter's moon was up. In New Mexico any moon means light you can read by, and I could see, in the last glimmer of light, the small sneaker tracks of my daughter as they wandered among the owl holes. She must have been just out of sight, hiding from me. I called for her again to let her know this was no time to fool around. Then I took off after the tracks that wavered in and out of the hills of trash. They wandered down behind the owl strip into a narrow arroyo.

And now real fear, which I had commanded to stay at the bottom of my thoughts, came to the top in a rush. I was in a panic that superseded reason; I ran at a fast sprint down the arroyo. Fifty feet ahead of me I saw her sitting in a blue-gray pool of moonlight and juniper shadow. She acted as if it were daylight, scooping sand, playing by herself. When she saw me running, she hopped to her feet and gave me one of those great vice-grip hugs.

"Daaa!" she shouted ecstatically, "I saw that owl."

"For Christ's sake, why didn't you answer daddy? I was going crazy calling for you."

She turned her head coquettishly.

"There's a mommy cow," she said. "And baby cow. And daddy cow."

"What cows? I don't see any cows."

She pointed ahead to a lump in the sand.

At first I couldn't make it out; it looked like a chunk of brown topsoil that had fallen off the top of the arroyo and dumped itself down on the sand. But then I saw the tail.

"Daddy, do cows have eyes?"

"Yes, of course they have eyes. What is that thing over there?"

How insane, I said to myself, my three-year-old sporting off into the moonlight to talk to owls and cows. She wasn't afraid. I was the one who was upset. I had broken into a cold sweat. I kept turning around to see if anything was behind me. Meanwhile, Hannah was tugging at my pants.

"It's the daddy cow. Mommy and baby went home. Have to wait for daddy cow to wake up."

"Oh, hell, Hannah, you and your spooky cows. Let's go home."

But a part of me, a big part, had an irresistible urge to have a look at what I now knew to be a carcass. Dumps were practical places for dead cows, though, and there was nothing unusual about seeing one here.

"I wanna see daddy cow 'gain," Hannah cried.

"Up we go," I said, picking her up. "No more cows tonight, wait until mommy hears what you've been up to!"

"Don't care," she answered in defiance.

I churned up the arroyo's steep bank, heaving with the weight of heavy little Hannah, and managed to reach the flat dump with strenuous effort.

An owl skimmed by my head so close I could feel the breath of its wings. Hannah squealed with glee.

"There goes that owl. Home to bed. Daddy cow sleeping now. He turned off his eyes, but he turned them on for me. Didn't he, Daddy?"

I put her in the front seat of the pickup and slammed the door on the driver's side after I had gotten in. The engine turned over the moment I switched on the ignition and I ground it into reverse.

"What did you say Hannah?"

"Cows don't have eyes," she said, "but they do."

We were passing the place where the cow had been, and I turned the wheel sharply to the right, cranked the emergency brake on, and put the floor shift in neutral.

"You stay put!" I threatened. "Or daddy will spank you hard!"

The truck's engine roared at high idle as I got out into the fountain of dust churned up by my sudden stop and peered down into the crevice.

Down in the gully I saw it. The biggest bellied dead cow in the world. And a couple of feet away from it, sitting in the place where I'd found Hannah playing in the sand, was a snow white dog the size of a lobo wolf. It was sitting there obediently as if waiting for dinner to be served.

I had the urge to hit it with a rock. Dogs have done many of the things imputed to wolves over the centuries. Mistreated feral dogs that run loose in the mountain towns of New Mexico are common and very dangerous. Hannah had been down there only moments earlier playing in the sand! I bent down to pick up a clod of dirt to scare it away, but when I looked again, the big dog was gone.

Then I looked again at the dead cow and saw what I had missed the first time. I ran back to the truck, threw it in gear, and spun off down the road.

What had it been? What had I seen? I couldn't be sure. I couldn't be at all sure I had really seen anything more than a dead cow and a white dog. But Hannah said it for me as we rounded the next hill toward home.

"The fireflies come out his eyes didn't they, Daddy?"

"Yes, they came out of his eyes."

"And out his mouth, too."

"Yes, there, too."

"But he didn't have a tongue. Poor daddy cow, he couldn't say words without a tongue. So the fireflies talked for him. Didn't they, Daddy?"

"Yes, they talked for him."

All the way home I kept seeing that white dog, the translucence of its fur, the light coming off it and out of the open mouth of the cow—the same light. The two of them exchanging bodies of light; the living taking from the dead. Or the dead from the living, which was it? I knew then that my best bet was to keep this strange thing I had seen a secret.

Part One

Prejudices

1

I was not someone who was good at keeping secrets, either for myself or for others. I had a tendency to talk. In fact, I loved to spill the beans. I'd pour out my troubles or sing like a canary when the going was tough. It was my way of releasing tension. That was probably why I had become a poet in the first place. My fantasy was to teach in some posh junior college in California, where I could wear comfortable slacks, smoke a pipe, and write poetry. For several years before moving to New Mexico, I was poet in residence at an eastern university and loved every minute of it.

Then a change took place. With the birth of my second child, I got the urge to get out of the East altogether. My poetry seemed trite, my comfortable life like a pair of shoes that had shrunk two sizes too small overnight. I broke off friendships, became irritable, and sandbagged a couple of worthwhile book projects. Clearly, I was burning my bridges, and for no apparent reason.

I worried endlessly if I was any good at anything. I took to reading books on Zen, began weightlifting at the local gym, and somehow, through all this sudden madness, decided to move West at the earliest opportunity.

I bought a two-seater Ford pickup, planned a route to the coast, and with no job, no secure future, hit the road with a two-month-old baby, a six-year-old, a wife, two dogs, and three cats. The animals rode in the rear of the pickup and panted through some of the worst July weather the country had ever known. In the summer of '76, Texas was a frying pan. We smuggled our cats into every motel. They crawled up the curtains to perch like parrots above the windows. From there they glowered at us until dawn when we hit the road again.

No wonder, then, traveling with all those animals and moaning little ones, that we ended our journey, partly from sheer exhaustion and partly because we felt we had found an oasis, when we came to Santa Fe, New Mexico.

From the sale of property in New England, we bought a small parcel of land and built an underground adobe house. I summoned my brother from where he was making a living as a studio musician, and my cousin, who was a contractor. With the two of them working alongside me, we laid the adobe bricks in six months. When the house was livable, I set out to find a job, or I should say, *jobs*, because I took whatever was available. I was a hod-carrier for another adobe crew, edited a magazine on southwestern boom towns, and spent eight months freelancing for the *New Mexican*, the oldest newspaper in the West.

Then I applied for a position on the staff of the *New Mexico Review*, a weekly magazine that printed political and art-oriented features. It was managed by a wizard of a man from Mississippi who had the slowest of southern manners and a brain like a buzz saw. So, I had what I wanted: a house and a job with a future.

It felt good to be back in New Mexico. I had been a college student at New Mexico Highlands University, a school that boasted an ethnic balance of Chicanos, Indians, and Anglos. While a student, I met my wife, Lorry, and made friends with both Navajo and Pueblo Indians. Shortly after college I spent a year working as a social worker on the Navajo Indian Reservation. I was suitably equipped to handle the job except for my distaste for bureaucracy, which eventually caused my departure to back East.

One evening in 1968, just before I quit working for the tribe, my wife and I were taking a walk up a lonely canyon road when a motorcyclist barrelled out of nowhere. Miraculously, the thing missed Lorry, but there I lay like a broken zither, discordant music playing in my brain, my right leg looking smashed beyond repair, my body in a pool of blood and splintered glass, and the cyclist spinning off again into nowhere.

I was taken to Santa Fe in an air splint. Emergency surgery saved my leg, but left me a partial cripple. Nine months in a cast and I could walk. The kid who hit me was given a citation for having a nonworking headlight, and fifteen months later he was killed in a gunfight in a northern New Mexico saloon. By then I was back in the ivy of New England reciting my poems to anyone who'd listen.

My past has a way of coming back to me when something in the immediate present shakes me by the roots. The anguish of that moonless, starless night when tires careened came back to me in a flash when I saw the clipping service bulletins spread out on my desk at the *New Mexico Review* that Monday morning after the dump run. The one with the loudest headline read: "D. A. Urging Mutilations Probe." The incidents of the past few years had grown so grotesque that some high-minded official seeking reelection now had to roll up his sleeves and plunge headfirst into that backcountry blood and gore. Of course, a long, perverse train of reporters would follow him.

I felt the motorcycle coming back into my life. I felt its hot breath coming toward me. These clippings laid out neatly on my desk meant that I had been chosen to undertake this task for the *Review*. I had just become the Man on the Mutilations Scene. I could picture myself crouched under a rancid steer carcass with a camera, waiting for a UFO to appear on the horizon. I was not going to accept this assignment without a fight. Unannounced, I marched resolutely into the managing editor's office, and said, "What does all this mutilation crap have to do with my feature on chili and its relationship to the low incidence of heart disease in northern New Mexico?"

"Scrap that assignment," Jamie Atkins said with an inspiring grin. "On to bigger and better things, my boy."

"But I was all set to interview a cancer specialist at Los Alamos, a guy who thinks chili may literally burn out cancer cells in the intestines of rats."

Jamie Atkins smiled wearily. He knew that I shied away from the hard-core stuff, and that if I refused an assignment, I meant it.

"Listen, there's a lot of pressure on us to hit the subject of these mutilations hard. If we do our job well, the D.A. may be pressured into tagging some federal grant monies for a really thorough investigation. I'm sorry, Gerry, but you're going to have to scrap the chili number for the time being. This mutilation thing is on red alert."

"I don't understand why everyone's so excited. These things have been going on under our noses for years and no one's given a damn."

"There's talk today of a Senate investigation, and for the first time, a tribal authority at one of the pueblos is saying there is 'alien interference from aircraft unavailable to us.' That's an exact quote. I mainly want you to take this assignment because you don't want it. Resistance always keeps you on your toes. You'll hate the blood and guts of it, but you'll listen until you get it right."

2

A couple of days after getting my assignment, I was puttering around in the microfilm library at the *New Mexican* hoping to turn up an angle or two. I had remembered seeing one of the first New Mexico mute stories. "Mute" was the term fashionable with the press. I liked both its simplicity and understatement. It seemed to say that surrounding these unexplainable events was a shroud of doubt. It also said that in the minds of those witnesses who had arrived shortly after a mutilation, the activity was strangely nonviolent.

It is second nature to a reporter to be objective, always on the edge of skepticism. I had been trained to let the event speak for itself. But now I was assigned to cover an event that was essentially inarticulate.

Studying mile after mile of microfilm in a dark, airless room, I found myself sinking into the swarm of microdots so deeply that I traveled into those black holes where the only sound was the hum of the screen. I was asleep with my eyes open.

"Sorry to disturb you," a voice said in the silence.

I woke with a start and peered at a tall form standing two feet away. I heard my voice rasp like a dry leaf scraping across a stone. "Who's there?"

"You look like a drowned man," came the reply.

Then I recognized the voice. It belonged to that implacable, earthbound old reporter named Robert Grundig. I would have turned impolitely back to my hypnotic viewing, but I needed him there at that precise moment.

He ambled up to my chair as I was recovering my senses and stared into the picture before me. It was a vintage shot of a mutilated heifer down by some pueblo creek bottom, two Indian tribal agents peering into its vacant mouth. The timeless halftone had an uncanny weirdness about it.

"Cheap trick," Grundig said. "Nothing to it."

Suddenly I resented his intrusion. His know-it-all, offhand, attitude bothered everybody who had ever bumped into him during an investigation. Even the police found him offensive and kept quiet around him.

"What do you mean trick," I said defensively, realizing the moment I said it that he had me.

21

"Elaine Eldridge took that shot and blew it with bad exposure. Don't tell me you, of all people, find that picture revealing of mystical truth?"

"I find it interesting, that's all. There's something about those Indians staring into the face of a dead cow—as if it might come back from the dead and talk to them. I find that damned interesting."

"Old hat. Our news bureau chief won't let any of us go near the story anymore. It's dead news. Forgive the pun."

"Your bureau chief must be a moron."

"Go ahead," he began, "tell me you see the light just wafting off the cow, and you'll be like those crazies from Taos who hung around that graveyard. What'd they call themselves—Druids? Yeah, that was it. Claimed they saw a blinking gravestone that was signaling the second coming. Well, I guess your rag prints that kind of stuff. Fortunately, I have better things to cover, like the reelection of Senator Dominguez, illegal payoffs in his last campaign drive—have a look at my one-pager on tonight's editorial page. Guaranteed to rattle some cages."

"Better make sure your own cage is clean first," I said as he walked out the door.

He pretended not to hear me. His feet clicked down the hall and I gathered up my things—pads of blank notepaper, the leather pony express bag I always carried on assignments, my favorite fountain pen, and some copies of clippings that had interested me.

That night I sat at home, as I knew I would, in front of a piñon fire popping with exploding sap, implosions deep inside the red coals in the black grate. Lorry sat beside me, our two children were already in bed. The house was quiet except for the wood popping and the wet wind blustering around the adobe house that was buried, all but the glass front, deep in the sandy ground.

On such a night you appreciate an underground house. I went outside to get more wood and the wind almost took my hat. I stared in the big front window at the cozy scene, my wife sitting before the fire pulling burrs out of the fur of our ten-year-old collie, who lay like a heavy sheepskin rug.

22

I liked the look of that house, the black brick floor with its zigzag pattern, the pueblo-style fireplace, set into the wall so that you could sit below it with the flames toasting your body and the whole wall. I would have given anything that night to get out of the newspaper business, write a thousand poems in front of that fireplace, and read them aloud once a night to my wife and the burr-ridden dog.

I knew well a familiar chemistry was working. My wife knew it too. As I came in with the wood she said, "You've got that look again. Don't tell me you don't, I can see it in your eyes."

"I had a funny kind of talk with Grundig today. You know how that grizzly son of a bitch gets me going with his smart-ass remarks."

"What did he say this time?"

"It's never what he says, it's how he says it. Oh, he got started on the mute business. Nothing heavy. I just didn't want to hear him mouthing off, especially when I'm so new on the project."

"That was the look you had when you first came home. It has nothing to do with Grundig, either. It's all you, the way you get yourself into things. I bet I know what's going to happen next."

"What?"

"You're going to try to get mutilated."

I forced a laugh but I knew it wasn't too convincing.

"Do I really look strung out already?"

She gazed quietly into the flames, and I wondered how she was able to keep her steady-as-she-goes attitude toward life.

"I suppose I'm willing to admit that this thing scares me a little," I said when she had lapsed into silence.

"What's there to be afraid of?" she said sarcastically, and then added wearily, "You always get like this. I guess I should be used to it by now."

"Used to what?"

"The 'it' syndrome. I've seen you fall in so many times I can't count them. I've waited for you to come back out and I'll do it again because I love you and I know you love me, but dammit, I hate you when you get 'it'—you're gone, that's all. Missing in action."

Her voice lost its urgency and trailed off. She too was hooked by

23

the flames, the way they were tangling themselves up like blue kitten's yarn in the back of the fireplace where the logs had fallen off and were absently smoldering.

"What's bothering you this time—what's different?" I asked.

"You."

"What do you mean?"

"I don't know. I'm worried—I can't figure it out. It's different, though. This time it's different."

"The hell of it is that you're always right. You know what Jamie said to me—did I tell you? He said, 'You'll hate the blood and guts of it, but you'll listen until you get it right.' Goddamn him for getting me into his dripping mess."

"You can't blame him. It's you. You're the one who gets sucked in."

"I got sucked up into a photograph today and I would still be in that microfilm library this very minute if Grundig hadn't busted in on me and interrupted my thoughts."

"Which were . . ."

"What was I thinking? Nothing. I was somewhere off in space with a floating cow."

"The cow that jumped over the moon?"

"The very one. Do you suppose that's the answer to the riddle?"

Outside the wind kept maneuvering under things, and a piñon branch steadily tock-tocked against the roof of our cave.

"To bed," I said. "I've had it with holy cows."

"No cows are invited, only cowboys," Lorry said, disappearing up the stairs.

3

There is a men's club in Santa Fe that dates back to the good old, bad old days of innocent literary loafing, when Witter "Hal"

Bynner was working on *The Jade Mountain*, his anthology of newly minted Chinese translations; D. H. Lawrence was busy twisting a version of New Mexico into a serpent that would twine down the ages; and a variety of poets, painters, and other roustabouts were busting up telephone poles because they blocked the view of their beer parlor. One testy old desert hump came to town with his best friend, who happened to be a brown bear but drank draft beer with the best of them. In fact, the bear was such a regular stench at the old La Fonda Bar that someone once poured a pint of perfume on its head while it slurped its daily ration.

This men's club, La Vida, has few members on its distinguished roster, but each has made a significant contribution to the world of letters, if not the unofficial *Guinness Book of Boozing*. Every month or so, when invited, I used to attend these once-a-month tipping sessions with a seventy-year-old doctor, who as a kid had run bets for Hemingway and his pals in Paris. An author and painter, he had been one of La Vida's founding members (along with Oliver La Farge, author of *Laughing Boy*, the great book about the Navajos that won the Pulitzer Prize in 1929).

On the Friday ending my first week on the investigation, the first of October, I was happy to put away my mute strategies, pick up a glass of bourbon, and hear talk about a time when things were more abundant and not nearly as serious—at least that was the way talk flowed at these get-togethers.

As we walked in the door of a high adobe built on a hill overlooking Santa Fe, we saw the author of several popular books and films. He was a gopher of a gentleman in his sixties.

"What are you writing these days, Jack," someone asked him offhand.

He raised his giant tumbler of whiskey in a salute: "Nothing. Nothing at all."

This brought the house down because all these merry old boozers wanted to do was booze, break wind, and make fun of the dreadful seriousness of life. They had had enough of writing and its demands, and wives and their demands, and besides La Vida was set up strictly for fun.

25

The moment I got there, I drifted in among the clusters of drinkers listening to this or that tale and getting pleasantly drunk myself, without the strain of having to introduce myself or even say a single solitary thing. La Vida was, for me, like going to the movies. I walked out the back patio door to admire the view of the distant mountains sparkling in the twilit smoke. There beside me with the regulation tumbler of bourbon in his crooked paw was old Grundig from the *New Mexican*.

"I thought this was a private club," he said drily, "but I can see they let in anybody who can slink up to the bar."

"Yes, that's right, anyone who can write ad copy and call it editorial can become a member nowadays."

"Well, don't let that discourage you," he said clattering the ice in his glass. "You'll write something yourself one day, and then you too will be invited to join."

I was about to make fun of his tie or his nose when I felt another presence and turned to see a man, somewhere in his early fifties, admiring the view with us. He was not drinking, or at least he had no drink in his hand, and that surprised me. I decided that he was a guest just like us, except that he didn't feel compelled to imbibe. He stood next to me staring into the sunset, a whisper of a smile on his lips.

"Twenty thousand people once lived on the other side of the river over in that valley," he said abruptly. "And now they're gone and the only trace of their existence is a potsherd or two."

" 'A splinter in the world's thought . . .' " I quoted.

"Yes," he said with a smile, "who was it said that—Jeffers, wasn't it?"

"That's right," and I felt a chill, not from the advancing darkness, but from the instant touching of two minds.

"Ever been over there?"

"No, not that exact location, but I've seen my share of ruins."

"Well, twenty thousand's a good number of people, and they had quite a civilization going for them. Peaceful folk, as you know.

26

We have no idea what made them move off, or where they went. They seemed to have vanished."

"My name's Gerry Hausman," I said, offering my hand.

"Carlton Murdock, from Los Alamos."

Through the haze of alcohol and relaxation broke the mute investigation I had come here to escape. The results of laser experiments at Los Alamos had recently been compared with burn marks that had been found on some mutes. A law enforcement officer covering the case had hired an assistant who had been a chemical technician both at Sandia Labs in Albuquerque, which did a great deal of weapons research, and at Los Alamos. His assistant had proclaimed that the only time he had seen such burn marks on animals was from metal burns from laser experiments at Los Alamos. The officer hastily added that no such equipment (capable of making incisions that were self-healing, bloodless, and practically absent of scar tissue) was "available to our government at this time." He claimed that the mutes were growing more and more sophisticated: no longer cloak and dagger stuff but highly technical operations.

Science fiction magazines were brimming with stories linking lasers to mutilations, but that was the first time a reputable source had made such claims. This could be my first behind-the-scenes break. I had just read a book about Los Alamos called *Fire on the Hill*. I asked Carlton if he had read it.

"No, can't say that I have," he answered, "but I don't read books about the present, only the past."

"What do you do over there?"

"I'm in the laser lab most of the time."

"That's a field I'm very curious about."

He chuckled. "Frankly, I'd rather chat about the Anasazi, myself. There's plenty of mystery there. Lasers, on the other hand, are a topic of finite dimension for me. Most people don't realize just how finite they really are; if they did, movies like *Star Wars* wouldn't make very much sense."

"By that I guess you mean the special effects were so overdramatized that they were scientifically laughable? I enjoyed the movie, whatever its incongruities might have been."

"All I can tell you, quite honestly, is that portable lasers, the destructive kind, are so far beyond our present capability that we can't even give them credibility as a futuristic dream—or science fiction nightmare, whichever one you prefer."

"Dinner is served," a voice commanded from the patio. "Come and get it, boys."

Carlton Murdock moved with the grace of a cat, a quiet confidence in his easy stride. Intrigued with the man and what he had told me, I was determined to find time during dinner or afterwards to question him further on the subject of laser beams.

Dinner was *posole* and pork—full-blown, watery, cooked kernels of corn steeped in chili and pork overnight until the white popcorn-looking corn kernels explode with the flavor of meat juice and soupy gravy. There were also side dishes of *carne adovada* or chili beef, the finest cut of beef in a rich red chili sauce flecked with little stars of burning red pepper. *Tortillas* and *sopapillas* completed the course. The tortillas were thick and spotted with brown pancake marks from the hot pan and the sopapillas, a Mexican version of the popover, were golden deep-fat fried wonders filled with honey. Both are considered excellent for dipping into the lakes of juice and pepper gravy left on the plate.

Card tables were set in three rooms of the long, low, adobe-style house. I would have preferred to eat outside in the dark and listen to October's last soldiers of the night, the crickets that refuse to give up in spite of the coming cold, but decorum called for a place inside with all the old men. I found Carlton seated opposite Grundig. That in itself demanded a trip to the bar before taking a place down from them at the same table. Altogether there were five of us eating there; the two others I recognized were a millionaire scholar-explorer and a columnist for the Luce empire during the fifties who had since retired to write his memoirs.

We were close-elbowed at that little table and probably that, and the tiring presence of Grundig, caused me to polish off two more tumblers of bourbon before I completed my meal. The chili burned—the old test proved it was really good stuff—burned going in and coming out. And the talk turned from one thing to another until the burly, bearded explorer squinted his eye, polished off a fifth of scotch with a swallow, grinned me down, and asked point-blank, "Well, what the hell do you do for a living?"

Everyone burst out laughing, including myself.

"I'm a cartographer," I said.

"The hell you say!" he said. "You're another damn writer like the rest of these bums!"

I admitted that I was and confessed for which paper, keeping a hawk's eye on Grundig because I was certain he was going to hook me with an embarrassing question.

"Hausman is the head of the *Review*'s new mutilation probe," he said, as lysergic acid dripped off his tongue and melted a hole in his tie. Then I did an uncharacteristic thing: I backed myself into a corner and told a big fat lie.

"Truth is," I yawned, "the whole subject is only days away from resolution. There have been a few recent leaks in the last week that will help me wrap it up much sooner than I expected."

Grundig swallowed some chili wrong and coughed violently. He tried to say something, but his voice came out old and scratchy, and he shut up and drank some beer to heal his throat. The other faces at the table were magnetized in my direction. In fact, several tables had fallen silent to hear what was coming next. Good, I thought, I've got their attention, now let's sock 'em in the shorts.

"It seems," I began, "that a couple of kids in Kansas have admitted to being part of a nationwide conspiracy to overthrow the government by attacking the meat industry. They, and others like them, have been perpetrating these crimes to cattle in the dead of night, using hip-pocket lasers that look like flashlights. Members of this secret task-force group have been picked up in Nebraska, Missouri, and parts of New Mexico. We've got a couple down in Belen awaiting trial, and my interview with them is to appear in print early next week."

I had intended to get out a few sentences of truth from last week's clippings. Then my head seemed to come off my shoulders and my mouth moved of its own accord and I said all these things that I had no desire to say, but then I was drunk as a skunk. What could I do now but keep from laughing? I bit my lip and looked at the blank faces. There was not a smirk in the bunch. My God, they'd taken it all in! I had said my bit so convincingly—because I had intended to be really sincere—that everyone in the room had given their attention to my pronouncement. I was a hero; I could see it in their eyes. I was the new bright boy reporter, the Nader of the mute scene. I was also a liar.

To break the silence, I coughed into my napkin and got up to get some more posole. At once, mumbled conversations started up. The sweat stood out on my forehead in silver drops, and the back of my neck burned. I scooped some more of the unwanted stuff into my plate and considered ducking out the patio door and disappearing forever into the night like the Anasazi.

At my side was Carlton Murdock. His hands were jammed into his front pockets, his chin thrust out like a bulldog. He looked menacing and mean, his eyes consumed with self-righteous anger.

"I want to talk to you outside."

He whipped around like a drill sergeant and left the room. My hands were shaking when I set down my plate. I grabbed my whiskey tumbler, gave it another copious fill, and headed out the door to meet the wrath of the concerned scientist. I had liked and admired this man the moment I met him, but now I had quite irrevocably offended him. No doubt, he was about to give me a piece of his mind that I would never forget.

He was back where we had first talked. The silence lay deep as folds in a blanket and the crisp air shone in the autumn moon.

His back was toward me. I came up quietly, my teeth set for the abuse that I deserved. When he faced me, I saw at once my drunkenness had the better of me again. This man wasn't mad; he was doubled up with laughter.

"That was great, wonderful," he said at last. "You knocked them

30

dead. They'll never give you a hard time as long as you live. You are one of them now, that's a fact."

"I'm not sure I did the right thing. I'm a little confused."

"Drunk's a better word."

"Yeah, I'm drunker than I ever intended to be. In the morning I think I'm going to regret that worse than anything."

"You'll survive. I can't get over how that one bully-boy, what's his name . . . the one with the white beard at our table who looks like Hemingway . . ."

"George Fielding?"

"He is the one. How you nailed him! He was all set to grill you and serve you up for a second course, but you popped him on the bean. Good show. What made it all believable was making the whole thing the effort of a bunch of crazy kids trying to kick over the government. Well, that's one thing these guys like to hear. They may seem like lovable old rascals or even lovable old radicals, but they're as conservative as Ronald Reagan."

He looked at his watch. "Time for me to go. Tell you what. Since you want to link the mutilations to laser beams, how would you like to see for yourself why it can't be so?

"Here's my card. I don't work tomorrow, but I have to be in my office to do some paperwork so why don't you call around ten and I'll meet you in town and bring you in at the security gate so you can take a look at one of those little lasers for yourself."

The moon was beating on my head, the voices in the house were back to surf crash volume, and tomorrow morning I was to go to the forbidden city on the hill to see firsthand why a laser beam couldn't cut up a cow. I hoped I could get sober before the sun came up.

4

To be awake and alert, I was up at dawn. Though to put it another way, I hadn't really slept at all, but rather had tossed fitfully through the night, wishing I was not aboard a pitching ship. At the first steely cold light, I needed no further excuse. I made some coffee, took a few voracious gulps, which burned my tongue and caused my stomach to roll, and went outside to breathe cold air and invigorate the blood.

All four of our disreputable curs greeted me at the door, with frosty breath and frozen paws. They guessed right; I was going for a run. I headed down the arroyo at top speed, feeling the congestion and smoke of the night before gather in my head and chest. My legs became pulpy and sore immediately, even though I exercise regularly. Debauchery is bad, I thought, and kept hammering at the sand with my sneakers, the shock in my knees lessening.

At the fifth ponderosa, I knew I had gone a mile and it was time to rest unless I felt up to the ridge run, yet another mile along the crest of the hill overlooking the deep scar of the arroyo. You have to feel like a little punishment when you take the uphill ridge run, but the commanding view of the Tesuque Valley, a good deal of the Pojoaque Valley, and the startling vision in salmon and mauve of Los Alamos waking as the rising sun hit it, was worth every bang of toe and heel.

The air on the ridge was iced with ether and had a hard kick. Halfway home, I was stopped by two things: the vast implication of the view and my laboring heart. I finished with that loose-legged walk that wayward, broken-field runners have when they suddenly stop after a long effort, or as in my case, a big night with the bottle.

Over toward Los Alamos I saw the hulking mesas of the San Ildefonso Indians. The sun's blood was all over Los Alamos. That place had been on my mind since my first visit to New Mexico: the hill city that spawned the bomb. Although Murdock had denied the mystery of lasers, I couldn't accept that, nor the greater mystery that encircled Los Alamos.

One night I had seen a globe, like the fiery tip of a glassblower's wine goblet, emerge from the snowy peaks behind Los Alamos. It had grown large and furry orange, risen to a height in the sky, and then, poof, disappeared. Lots of peculiar things happened at Los Alamos all the time. Not long ago, two men cleaning a vat in one of the labs had suddenly been asphyxiated and dropped dead. Scientists, from time to time, committed suicide, their secrets dying with them as they extinguished themselves and their work. A maximum security check taking a year was required for any employment position on the Hill, even for janitors and secretaries. Yet, the most chilling fact about the city was not its secrecy, but what it had once given to the world. In the middle of mountains and primitive religion, a bomb was born that may yet put out the world. Walking home, sweat freezing on my temples, I knew that I had not, and probably would not, attempt to make peace with my true feelings about Los Alamos. Despite attempts to keep a professional objectivity, I was in the dim camp of my worst prejudices.

Could the men who gave us the bomb be at work on a swifter, more precise weapon of ultimate destruction? It was the poetry of violence that appealed to me, not its reality. Let it be real and all was lost. At this point in my mind, the mutes were a peripheral truth. I would consider the poetic truth of all things, the more unsupportable the better.

I went back in my mind to the night at the dump. I had left the scene almost immediately, not staying long enough to fully take it in. It wasn't only because of the child. Something inside me demanded the mute theme stay mute, undiscovered, unattended by human wisdom. Perhaps this was why I could casually take a drive to Los Alamos with childish wonder ballooning in my mind like that surreal globe of light.

I got to Los Alamos by around nine-thirty and phoned Carlton Murdock from a diner at the edge of town. "Town" is a cluster of

33

prefab, military-gray buildings hastily constructed for a hasty purpose. A sterility enters the blood on reaching the outer limit of Los Alamos.

My call to Carlton went through a couple of extensions but finally reached him at his desk. Although the connection was loud and clear, the man sounded like somebody else. I asked if I was speaking to Carlton Murdock and identified myself as the brash reporter of the night before. He cleared his throat and said formally that I must wait where I was until he returned my call in a few minutes.

"I repeat," he said, "stay where you are until my return call."

I sat at the counter of the diner, looking over my shoulder at the phone. Trying to ward off the tremors of alcohol-headache that had been with me from the moment I opened my eyes, I had almost finished a second cup of coffee when the phone rang. I leaped out of my seat, causing a number of people at the counter to stare. What a flair for the dramatic I have these days, I thought.

It was Murdock. "Stay put. Someone will meet you in a couple of minutes. What are you wearing?"

"Red ski vest. Should be easy to see me; I'll be outside in the parking lot, okay?"

"I'd rather you stayed in the diner, if you don't mind."

"Alright with me. I'll . . ."

He clicked off. I went back to the counter and ordered a refill; at least I'd be wired when the someone came to get me. This was sort of what I had expected. What did puzzle me was Murdock's official manner. Could he have changed that much overnight? Then I realized that at first impression he had not looked like a scientist at all. He had acted like the other writers in La Vida, only less hell-bent to get smashed.

Then there was that moment at the posole bowl, when Murdock had come over with unmistakable anger in his eyes. Outside, when I saw him again, he had been friendly and easy. I had completely eclipsed the rude face at the posole bowl. In the logic of drunken people, why remember that someone *seemed* mad at you, when in fact, this was proven not to be the case?

34

I felt a gentle hand on my shoulder. A large man wearing green fatigues, a quilted gray work-jacket, and a duckbilled, redneck's cap was standing over me. He had a big smile on his face, which was friendly and outgoing. He looked like a garageman with big hands and big ears.

"I thought you were who you were. I'm your pickup," he said, scratching his bald head nervously with his cap off.

We got into a gray Ford marked with LASL, United States Department of Energy, and a contract number of about six digits with a code in letters. So far so good. I relaxed in the company of my pickup man. I assumed that I was one of many routine pickups.

"Nice weather," he said, grinning like Davy Crockett.

"Couldn't be better."

"Say, how classified is the place where we're going?"

"It's classified. That's why they sent me to get you. But if it were real classified even I couldn't go near it. No one goes near *that* building, for instance."

We had already passed into the main complex, but there had been no screening points. He had gestured to a cinder block structure surrounded by a highwire fence. I felt like I was in a spy movie.

"What's in that building?"

"Couldn't tell you. I mean, even if I knew, which I don't."

"Lots of secrets here, I guess."

"You're about to walk inside one."

We came to a huge fenced parking lot, and a guard appeared in the entry booth. At the end of the lot were nondescript brick buildings, new foundations, and cheap duplexes with the usual asbestos shingle exteriors.

The attendant at the main gate nodded to my driver, who showed his plastic-coated pass. The guy in the booth took a good look at me and then nodded to both of us. What if I had had a bomb in my pocket? Would the guard have seen it with bionic X-ray eyes?

We pulled up to a seventy-foot-long, white mobile home which had another of those security fences. On the steps of the trailer was Carlton Murdock. He looked the same, but clipped to his lapel was a plastic pass with his mug shot and serial number. He was standing as stiff as his voice had been on the phone.

I wanted to keep appearances from deceiving me. I greeted him with my mellowest hello and warmest handshake. He returned it with a cold nod and a deadfish shake. He was definitely not the same man. He escorted me to the inside of the trailer, which was appropriately paneled in fake wood. The narrow office filled with rows of secretarial desks and filing cabinets looked like a wind tunnel.

"Come into my office, please," he said, still affecting the aloof demeanor. When he turned his back, I saw his shoulders twitch nervously. His office told another story altogether. On the walls were posters from the Sierra Club and photographs of redwoods and lichen. That was the man I had met at La Vida, not this upset diplomat. He took a seat behind his desk and I sat opposite.

"Coffee?" It was his first civil gesture.

"Thanks, no, I'm coffee'd out. That was some party last night, wasn't it?"

I wanted to determine the accessibility of the eight- to ten-hour-old past.

"You'll have to excuse me," he said wearily, rubbing his eyes with his fingertips. "I didn't sleep at all last night, and I was under considerable fatigue just from being at that party."

"I meant to ask you what member you came with . . ."

"No one invited me. I came uninvited. With permission, of course."

He looked grayer, older, and more like the spineless creature that should inhabit the cold, oppressive buildings that filled the view out his office window.

"On assignment?" I cracked.

He manufactured a counterfeit of the counterfeit smile I'd seen last night.

"We appreciate your making this trip to see us," he said. "And that was our purpose in attending the party. It was, there is no getting around it, an assignment. To bring you here, of your own accord."

36

"Well, I'm here and of my own accord, so what's this all about?"

"You're new to the field, I take it? And I believe your paper is also rather new, isn't it? Your boss is a Mississippian, isn't he? Well, those things are neither here nor there. Our purpose is to show you what lasers can and can't do, and, most important, what we'd like them to do in the future."

His searching look almost returned him to the person he had been out on the terrace talking Anasazi.

"I didn't mean to scold a moment ago, but I had a hard time controlling myself last night. You were very much out of hand, were you not?"

"I was drunk. There's a difference."

"That's no excuse for immoral conduct."

"I wasn't aware of my immorality."

"Maybe we should give it another name, let's say your lack of discretion with regard to your profession. You made some rather portentous statements which were a discredit to your paper and yourself. You may have caused public embarrassment for some innocent people."

"You'll have to fill me in on the details. All I remember about last night is that you were in a good humor, while today you're not."

"We'd rather not delve into specifics, if you don't mind. Our purpose is to inform you that you were treading on thin ice. And also to acquaint you with what we do here in this department. Am I being clear?"

"So far. Is it possible for you to get to the point? I am not a dolt, you know."

"That is not my job, I'm afraid. I was asked to bring you here; the rest is for my superior to handle. Thank you for your time, Mr. Hausman."

Obviously under considerable strain, he got his hat and coat and went out the door without so much as a good-bye. Well, hell's bells, I wasn't a criminal, was I? A dapper fellow entered on cue. He had a round, well-fed, midwestern face that spoke of corn-fed beef and good times fishing at the creek.

"I am Ronald Ambersand," he said jovially, "and I intend to give you a tour here this morning. You must forgive Mr. Murdock. He is our local information officer, under my jurisdiction. I am in charge of all informative releases to the public from all divisions of LASL."

"I am sorry if I was a nuisance last evening. Mr. Murdock seems to think I blundered into sacrosanct territory."

"Well, in fact that is just what you did. But I don't feel any real harm was done. Mr. Murdock, you know, isn't entirely suited for his job. There are occasions where he feels put-upon to accept little assignments like that party. He's quite a loner, really. It should suffice to say to you that speaking too candidly about things you know nothing about is, at the very best, indiscreet. Shall we get on with the tour, then?"

As I had expected, the tour was a streamlined pass through unclassified areas of laser experimentation. The machinery was highly technical, and I was impressed the same way I had been impressed with the planetarium in New York as a kid. After showing me through the bunker-like shop where laser hardware was being designed and executed for experiments, he let me poke my hand into a harmless laser beam that made a red dot on my skin, but was otherwise undetected by my nervous system.

"What we're working on here," he droned, "is the potential of using lasers to fuse atomic nuclei in a controlled manner to release energy. You see, the energy of the sun itself is the result of thermonuclear fusion—two light elements colliding, fusing to form a heavier element, and in the process, releasing energy.

"Now, the idea behind laser fusion is to manufacture a small sphere, a pellet of glass, or we can call it a microballoon. It is actually one hundred to two hundred micrometers in diameter. To clarify the visual image, you can sit a number of them on top of a hair follicle, which magnified, would like like a log. Am I making myself clear to you?"

"I have read about microballoons," I told him, "and I already know that they are filled with a deuterium and tritium mixture, an earthly equivalent of the reaction taking place on the sun."

"Well, I can see you have done some homework, very good. Most reporters couldn't care less about these things."

I was writing a sci-fi thriller in my head. There were lots of lasers and little men like Ambersand blowing kingdoms into kingdom come. I had a good seat up front for the whole show.

". . . a short pulse of laser light," he was saying.

I envisioned a great dome of inner space rolling through the starlands. Presto, that short pulse of laser light . . .

". . . this light takes only a nanosecond, strikes the fuel pellet, and is absorbed by the outer layer . . ."

. . . exploded my brain and . . .

"This absorbed light causes the outer layer to vaporize and blow away as a hot plasma."

. . . then the pulse of power the earth and stars knew would come from man one day, oh, I could see it all, the final umbilical cord cut to . . .

"An inward rocket-reaction force compresses fuel in the center of the pellet and heats it to the fusion reaction temperature, and the DT fuel undergoes fusion burn."

Nothing can stop the head-over-heels plummet to the end of life as we know it, caused by a quick pulse of . . .

". . . light, yes, if you've been following me, each laser pulse could contain, for example, one megajoule of energy, enough to run a color television for one hour!"

"For one whole hour?"

I acted bowled over by this preposterous fact. Actually, it was more than a trifle depressing. I had been blowing up solar systems and here he was talking about operating a puny TV set.

"What about the ultimate implications of this effect on weaponry—on the military for instance?"

His eyes turned into tiny time capsules pulsing with laser light.

"You persist, don't you, Mr. Hausman? You won't let civility be your guide. I was just about to show you the classified lab where our Antares project is presently housed. Now I'm not sure I should."

"I'm sorry about getting hung up on the military all the time. My background, I guess." I meant the apology sincerely. "You have to understand something," I went on, "I'm from another generation. I grew up on Flash Gordon, Buck Rogers, Captain Midnight. I thought *Star Wars* was a documentary."

He gave me a wisp of a smile, like his predecessor.

"Look," I said, "you're prejudiced against me because you think I'm prejudiced against you. We're not communicating at all. What I'm really curious about *is* the military implication. I want to hear categorically what is possible and what is out of the question. That's what I need to know for my job."

"Alright," he said, "I will trust that you are sincere this time and merely curious, and I will show you why it is illogical to imagine that the laser handguns that you read about in all the magazines could ever approach feasibility."

We walked very fast to a large, creamy yellow cinder block building. A flag flew on its roof, and wide stairs led to its doors. We entered through glass doors and a uniformed, armed man met us at the main desk.

Mr. Ambersand showed his badge, the man jotted down the serial numbers on a clipboard file sheet.

"Would you please make out a temporary visitor's pass for this gentleman?" Ambersand asked.

The officer appraised me with the fixated eyes of someone who has seen too much television. He put my driver's license into an apparatus, pushed a green button, and instantly, I, too, had a badge of entry into the most secret cellar of Los Alamos. We entered an elevator on our right and descended into the depths of the building. We landed in a vast chamber that looked like a vast boiler room, swollen with great bulbous pipes and confusions of wire and tubing. The workers were wearing puffy orange playsuits and white plastic boots. I felt sufficiently humble.

40

"Please put on a pair of those overshoes," Mr. Ambersand said. "They help keep dust and foreign matter out of the laser facility."

We walked into a smaller laboratory chamber similar to the last one, but here the laser equipment was gigantic—operative. The entire space was filled with a series of lathes lined up on a huge table interspersed with mirrors to direct the light pulse.

"This whole thing is operated upstairs by computer. There it goes," he added enthusiastically.

I heard a bzzt and a click, and it was over.

"There is an eight-beam system," he said, "the most powerful CO_2 laser in the world. Our goal here is scientific break-even, that the energy released by the pellet fusion reaction equals or exceeds the laser pulse energy that strikes the pellets. In the future, we may be able to turn over our whole concept of electricity. You may be looking at the power source of the future. *I* believe you are, anyway. Now do you see why this application is nonmilitaristic? Come here, just a second, will you?"

He led me out the door, down a corridor, and through another door into a cavernous place dominated by the biggest cylinders in the world. Iron circular stairways led to platform stations where lab technicians were poking into the mouth of one of the reaction chambers. One of them said, "Some of these pellets are dead as doornails." I couldn't make out what his partner said. It was impossible to be in this cavity without wondering what it all meant, and whether Ambersand was right about the future of the world. It was equally impossible to comprehend that within the immense reaction chambers were pellets or microballoons that were handmade, not constructed by a machine, yet were so small that one could fit into the eye socket of the eagle on a quarter.

As we left the building into the bright New Mexico sun, I could see the piñon-spotted hills below the Sangre de Cristo's, which any day would be dusted with snow, and the rumpled rug country of valleys and arroyos that was my home. They were so dreadfully close to all this impersonal supersonic pellet madness.

Too close, I thought as I shook Ambersand's hand and got into my transport vehicle. Ambersand seemed so delighted with himself for having blown off the top of my head with the Antares Project that I wanted to deflate him.

"There is one thing I wanted to ask, if you don't mind."

"Go right ahead."

He looked wary, but was clasping his hands in excitement like a dean on graduation day. I was sitting comfortably in the front seat of the grayish transport. My driver was a newly coined smiler just like his earlier look-alike.

"How does the fact of Antares negate military application?"

His face fell. He turned crimson. His hands clenched into fists at his side. Then he remembered his diplomatic mission with the outerworld. In his eyes I was another hopeless writer.

"I will tell you only one thing, young man," he said bitterly. "If you could find a way to install a unit the size of Antares in an aircraft, you would then be in a position to put a battleship into a handgun."

"I think that finally answers my question."

5

The road from Los Alamos has been blasted, hand-hewn, and hammered down a series of steppes. The price of the view is cliff-hanging around corners and looking over sheer precipices and the spikes of ponderosas hundreds of feet below. The lack of any sizable guardrails stimulates images of freefalls to oblivion.

Slowly I wound my way down, hugging the roadbed opposite the cliff, and thinking serene thoughts of my next experience if my brakes should fail or the steering wheel come off in my hands. Halfway down to terra firma, I noticed a flashing police car right behind me. I knew I couldn't get a ticket for speeding going ten miles an hour on curves, but those red flashing lights coming out of nowhere made me break out in a sweat.

I drove at an infuriatingly slow pace until the scenery turned to a picture postcard of gold cottonwoods and scattered adobes, unplastered with the rain-streaked bricks showing. In fifteen minutes, I had gone from the desperation of the future to the sandscapes of the ancient past. I was safe.

Then my attention returned to the police car still blinking at me in my rearview mirror. My paranoid fantasy had come true; the ruby lenses had blinked only for me all the way down the mountain. I pulled far over on the gravel shoulder and got out to meet the cop on neutral territory.

He was a medium-sized man, built like a boxer with a handsome face and dark Indian eyes. Accompanying him was a gawky figure wearing a long, black, leather overcoat. They didn't look like they belonged together.

"Was I driving too fast?" I asked the officer.

"Routine check," he said coughing into his fist nervously.

It was the tall man who moved hesitantly in the direction of my '78 Subaru station wagon.

"May I please see your license?" the officer said in a heavy Spanish accent. I had not heard that rich mountain inflection of Spanish in a long time. The language of colonial Spain around the time of Cabeza de Vaca had stuck in the hinterlands of northern New Mexico up near Chama.

"Routine, just routine," he said again as he glanced at the license like it was just another horned toad on a rock. He handed it back to me with obvious disinterest and cocked his head toward the other guy, who was going through the kiddie things in the back of the stationwagon.

43

"What the hell does he think he's doing?" I asked the cop, who appeared to have the same reaction.

"Hey," the cop shouted, "Kreuger, what the hell you doin'—checking his laundry or something?"

The man climbed out of the back of the little car shaking his head between those two sharp hawk's shoulders. He halfheartedly offered his hand.

"I'm Len Kreuger. Sorry for all this."

"I can't accept your apology, Mr. Kreuger, until I find out what this was all about."

Kreuger looked from me to his compatriot, then back. He dug into the leather coat for a crumpled cigarette pack. His hawk features were even more exaggerated now close up.

"Tell him," the officer said.

Kreuger scanned the outlying cliffs over the Rio Grande, as if to prepare himself for a sudden flight.

"I am a retired agent of the FBI," he told me. "I had no business doing what I just did. If you sued me tomorrow, I'd be up shit's creek."

"I wouldn't go that far," the officer said, suppressing a smile.

"I didn't do it for kicks, however," Kreuger added defensively.

"Then what did you do it for?" I asked.

"Gomez here got a call that you had been agitating one of the laser specialists up at the labs. Ambersand was the name I think he gave, and he made it clear that you might have picked up something that didn't belong to you."

"Now don't get off on that remark," Gomez said to me. "Some of those scientists up there are as nutty as the next guy."

"Nuttier," Kreuger said.

"I should have expected this."

"Hey," said Gomez, "don't take it personal. Neither one of us said you took something that didn't belong to you. We did our job, and that's where it ends."

"I think there's more to this than you're telling me. Besides, why, pray tell, is an ex-FBI agent cruising with a state cop who is a

44

hundred miles from his station at Dulce—I couldn't help noticing your badge."

Gomez didn't seem to resent this line of reasoning. In fact, he found it funny. Kreuger perused the cliffs.

"That's the hell of it," Gomez laughed. "I see him once in a blue moon. We got together to have a look at a lab specimen that was brought here from Sandia Labs."

"What kind of specimen?"

"Who's doing the interview, anyway?" Krueger said.

"Maybe I am."

Now both men really saw me for the first time.

"What's your line of work?" Kreuger asked.

"I'm a reporter for the *New Mexico Review*."

"Shit," Kreuger said.

Now Gomez was scanning the cliffs, disinterested in both of us.

"I take it you don't care for the paper," I said.

"I don't care for any newspaper that prints lies. That describes most of what's on the stands—made my life miserable for twenty years. Well, what do I care, I'm out of it now.

"I didn't quit," Kreuger said to me confidentially. "I retired."

"He got old," Gomez said with a smirk. "Lost his nerve. Afraid he'd shoot off his foot."

Kreuger showed his teeth in a smile that was not forced.

"What if I had been found with a laser stethoscope that I was taking home to my kids," I asked. "What would you have done?"

"I would have taken it home to my kids," Gomez said.

Kreuger's laugh jerked his frame.

Gomez said, "Shit, Len, what the hell are we doing shooting the shit when we got work to do."

"You mean you got work to do. I'm retired, remember?"

"You quit just when it got interesting, Len. Now's the fun part."

"Some fun, chasing a bunch of dead cows someone thinks were mutilated by some maniac. That's fun alright."

"You two aren't covering the mutes are you? I'll bet you were up at the labs for a hide examination . . ."

"Look out, he's smart," Gomez said.

"Well, if he's as smart as he thinks he is, let him have a look at what you got in the back of the car," Kreuger said, spitting on the road.

"Hey, that's not a bad idea," Gomez said. "How about a picture for the paper? Let's get one with the two of us here and that thing propped up on the hood."

Gomez flung open the trunk and removed a zippered plastic bag. In the cold air, the bag was fogged and I couldn't see what was inside.

"Wouldn't that rip open some hearts, if they could see it like it really is?" Kreuger said.

Gomez unzippered the bag and bellied it open. I smelled a chemical like formaldehyde. Inside the bag was a cow's head, the mouth open and the tongue sticking out.

"That looks obscene," I said, rooted to the spot with morbid fascination. "But how come the tongue's all crooked like that?"

Kreuger did another one of those back-wracking laughs with his hands hidden in his pockets and the cigarette falling out of his mouth. Gomez was spanking his knee and laughing. It was too bad the subject of their amusement wasn't as amusing as they were.

I stared at the head. The fur was matted from the moisture in the bag. A familiar thing becomes surreal when it is seen out of context; a head is a head until it comes off a body, then it is something else. This head looked like it might speak. It looked intelligent and deserving of our attention on some intellectual plane. If the head could only talk.

I wondered what force could torque a tongue like a rubber band. Gomez put his hand on my shoulder. "Hey, buddy, if you think that's a tongue you better get your head in that bag and take a better look."

Suddenly it wasn't surreal. It was sickening. My whole body went light and loose, the two men next to me grew dim. I held onto the hood of the car with both hands and felt a wet vomit rise in my stomach.

Then the light was clear all around me. The two men were still there, and I knew only a couple of seconds had actually passed. I still did not know what the tongue was, but knew it did not belong there. I saw the head and the great globule of rotten twisted tongue. This animal had been tampered with in a horrible way. I thought of the Devil, of heads on spikes, of things that have no name but run on hooves of fear in the human blood and brain. For a moment, I felt connected to whatever it was that had made the head what it now was, and that made me monstrously ill.

I was conscious of Gomez staring at me.

"You okay, buddy?" he said.

"I'm okay. I got queasy there for a second."

"You see enough of these things, you don't think anything about it," Kreuger said. "There's nothing to this one, except that some idiot took that animal's dong and ran it up its throat and out its mouth. Then the son of a bitch twisted it and twisted it like metal on a forge."

"Don't that beat all," Gomez said. "How'd you like to have a *derga* for a tongue, Len?"

Kreuger didn't answer him. He was staring at the bag biting his lip thoughtfully.

"Animals don't do this kind of shit to other animals," he said. "They're too civilized."

"Even a monster wouldn't do it," Gomez said.

"I know one that would," I said. "They walk on two legs."

"That's about the size of it."

"Let's get on back to Santa Fe," said Gomez. "I got work to do."

6

"You were saying?" Lorry said that night at dinner.

"I'm sorry, I must have drifted off again. What were we talking about?"

"Something about that awful head."

"Oh, yeah. That pair of characters and that head and the whole affair up in Los Alamos make me wonder if I'm cut out for this assignment. This career, even. I should be doing something else."

"Like what?"

"I've always wanted to be a lookout for the forest service."

"You've also dreamed of being a sheep farmer, fruit picker, horse wrangler—and how could I forget, a writer. Come to think of it, you don't want to be anything but a writer when you're contented with your writing. The problem right now is that you don't want to write about cattle mutilations for another six months, and I don't blame you one bit. Neither would I."

"I'd make a great sheep farmer, up in Montana somewhere."

"You'd hate every blessed woolly second. Besides, sheep get mutilated, too, don't they?"

"They do at that. All kinds of critters get mutilated."

"What have you learned in the last week?"

"You mean what information have I gleaned with which I might proceed to niftily tie up the mute business and score the Pulitzer Prize in journalism?"

"Don't be clever. I'm serious."

"It's not a fair question. I've only been at it a week."

"Give me a week's worth of insight."

"I don't really know a hell of a lot, but I can tell you that they have been happening for a very long time. They're not new to this part of the country."

"How long?"

"Since the mid-sixties, anyway. There have been mutilations all over this country, and they are not restricted to livestock. Plenty of dogs have been found: cats, chickens, goats, and lots of horses. You know, the horse mutes are the most horrendous. I read about a horse that had its skin lifted right down to the nerves. They found it dead on its feet with no skin."

"That makes me want to puke."

"Now you know how I felt when I saw that head today."

"I take it back, Gerry. I don't want to know anything more about these mutilations. Not if they involve hurting horses. By the way, did you know another incident was reported in the papers today?"

"Another mute?"

"It happened a couple days ago. Just now got into the papers."

"That explains why Kreuger and Gomez didn't care if I saw that head. I thought it was a little odd that they just opened up their trunk and let me have a look."

"Apparently right now they want all the publicity they can get. Your man Kreuger said in the interview that he was considering coming out of retirement to organize a full-fledged, government-funded probe that will last more than a year."

"Old Kreuger is a funny kind of law enforcement officer."

"How do you mean?"

"He was a strange combination of easygoing, ruthless, serious, comic, and so on. He might be dangerous, if he were let loose on the case."

"I don't see why you have to be so closely involved. Maybe you could ask Jamie to let up on you."

"Our paper's not known for glossing over the facts."

"That isn't what I meant at all."

I recognized that green-eyed look. She was worried, and whenever she got that way, I got worried, too. Being the big provider, I was supposed to cover it all up with a smile and say, "Don't worry, dear, it's all in a day's work," and "How are the kids tonight?" But I'm not that kind of guy. I'm a progressive, liberal, left-handed worrywart. When I worry, buildings rattle, cracks open up in the sidewalk, and inevitably I quit my job.

I just go worry somewhere else. How many lives had I slithered out of, how many identities had I shed? Around the time of my accident, I had been so paranoid that I went to bed at night with a .38 revolver under my pillow, a light on, a radio blaring. Well, I wasn't about to get into that head trip right now, just when things were going good at my job. I was going to put up and shut up. Cattle mutilations were hot shit, and that was all there was to it.

"What is that noise?" Lorry said.

"I don't hear any noise."

"That. Don't you hear it? Listen."

The look on her face took me back more than ten years. I saw her sitting on a log in the moonlight, way up the Gallinas Canyon where the Penitentes were singing. It was Good Thursday and they were deep into their ritual of pain moaning and cactus whipping, but their song, carried to us on the wind, had a moonlit purity. When you trained your ears to pick up its sound, it was an untrammeled chanting, a nasal whine that came down the canyon on a spring wind. It was filled with youthful fears and longings—not of the Penitentes alone. I wanted to marry her then, as they sang in the dark pines. That same wild animal look was on her face now. It made me want her badly.

Then I heard the mechanical, unrelenting grinding. It was not the poetry of the Penitentes, but equally immeasurable. I got up and went to the window. It was happening down in the arroyo. I would have to put my coat on and go out and see what it was. How tiresome this was getting to be.

"Forget about it," Lorry said when she saw me head for the closet below the bedroom stairs.

"What do you mean . . . you're the one who made me listen for it. Now I have to see what it is, damn it."

I have to admit that a certain small part of me liked to see her frightened; a larger part, sicker most likely, enjoyed going out and playing the big hero of the night. We did this to each other on a

50

regular basis: she getting scared, me picking up on it, then both of us playing the martyr—Lorry huddling in a corner and me going out to face the beast of the crooked tree. Actually, the remote setting of our house, bordered on all four sides by national forest and Indian land, resulted in some pretty unexplainable night noises. Bears frequently came down the arroyo looking for autumn apples and coughed like old men right under the bedroom window. Coyotes, at first dark and always at dawn, yipped and yowled and carried on, and our dogs took off after their shadows.

Once or twice a year stranger things than varmints came up or down the arroyo. One time a low rider rumbled to within a few feet of the house. Low riders are varmints who haunt southwest roads in cars so low to the ground that you couldn't put a cigarette pack under the back bumpers. The driver wore a scarf around his head, the rest of his face was greasy and pimply. He endeavored to speak to me with lips that were fastened upon a toothpick. I was caught among fear, loathing, and fascination. He asked after another subspecies of his kind who was lost in the vicinity of our house. I told him I had seen no one anywhere near the property, which was true. Fortunately, that low rider was alone. But tonight I was relaxed after a good dinner Lorry had made and in no mood to find another of those thing-persons up to its axles in arroyo sand. Now our dogs were barking. I set foot into the frosty night. The dogs nipped playfully at my heels while running ahead and then coming back as they always did on my jogging expeditions. The noise heaved and grated now. As I got closer, it heaved forward and backward, as a car might rock if it were half sunk in sand.

The farther I went up the arroyo, the more I wondered how a vehicle of any kind, even one with four-wheel drive, could climb so steep an incline, not to mention traverse the hard rock cobble and avoid the overhanging limbs of the piñons. A coyote let out a fearsome yowl somewhere up the arroyo.

Now the noise changed in pitch to a gravelly beating sound. Chrrrr-click, chrrrr-click. Our big husky, Kita, took the chase seriously for the first time. She led the other dogs and left me far behind.

Whatever I was going to find at the end of this hike, I wanted to view it from a decided advantage. I trekked up the hill above the arroyo, easily reaching the top where I was able to see for some distance, even in the dark.

I surveyed the whole little valley encapsulated below. In the shadow of an immense shagbark juniper, a great white microbus was beached like the great white whale. It was one of those blimps that can go anywhere, get stuck anywhere, and cost a fortune to fill with gas. As I had suspected, a single tire was mired in the sand and working itself in to the axle. The air stank of rubber, thick smoke hung in the pools of light from the headlights.

My dogs were acting like they had treed this beast, and the driver inside was theirs to do with as they pleased. How, I asked myself, did this cumbersome vehicle get up here? There was no road or feasible access, up or down.

I kicked the dogs out of my way as I came up to the light. Immediately, a voice called from the driver's side: "Get those god-damn dogs out of there."

They continued to bark at twenty feet or so, and the driver jumped out. He was about six foot six, dressed in a silver down jumpsuit like a super-fancy motorcycle outfit.

"How do you?" the man said as calmly as if he were stepping out of a subway car in Pelham Manor.

"How the hell did you get way up here in that thing?"

"Up by the microwave tower, there's a public service access road that was used for laying phone cable years ago. I took it and ended up here. That simple. But now I'm stuck up to my asshole."

"You can say that again. But I still don't get how you got from that access road, which is itself a bloody mess, to here, where there is no road at all."

Broken cactus arms were stuck to his tires, axles, and front bumper. He'd obviously karate chopped himself and his land blimp right through the badlands until there was no way out but up. He was a brave dummy.

"What possessed you?"

"You mean drive way the hell out here?"

"Yeah."

"We're surveying for Territorial Land and Cattle."

This statement set me back on my heels.

"At night? In a national forest?"

"I admit to being temporarily off course. But I was okay at noon up there by the tower."

"Noon, you say? That means you've traveled about three miles in eight or nine hours?"

"Affirmative."

He looked at the ground.

"Lots of schist in this area," he said, changing the subject.

He looked and acted military: abrupt, swift movements, crew cut, kamikaze assignment. No one except a soldier, an escaped prisoner, or a government agent would dare to accept so ignoble and ludicrous a task as hacking through a cobweb of cactus and juniper to an unnavigable arroyo. Territorial Land and Cattle, my ass. I decided that the best I could offer him was a walkabout to where the arroyo turned into a dirt road that led to the Rio Encantado Dude Ranch. Digging him out was out of the question, and I didn't want him anywhere near my own house.

"Come on," I said. "I'll show you the way out on foot."

"Nothing doing. I'm not about to leave this station."

"What station?"

"My vehicle station. My equipment's in it."

"I see. Well, I guess you have other plans for getting back to civilization."

"Dig out and keep moving."

"Dig out . . . you must be joking. You're not going anywhere unless by airlift."

"Affirmative. I have a call in now. I'll be on my way in no time."

Now I knew he was off his rocker. There was also no doubt that he belonged to a military reconnaissance mission. The dogs continued to maintain their distance. Usually they came up once the enemy had been proven to be just another harmless smell in the universe. Something about this guy put them off, as it did me. Aside from burnt rubber, he smelled like something—maybe ammonia. In a ring around the vehicle, the dogs sat positioned for a surprise thrust. I gave Kita a fake kick from ten feet away, and she backed off into the night with a low growl.

"I'd muzzle those dogs if I was you," the man said.

"Wouldn't think of it."

"I would if I were you," he threatened.

"Well, it's back home, then, for me. Glad I could be so much help." But as I turned to go, Burke, our half-blind Doberman, dove out of the dark like an assassin and sank a fang into the giant's left leg. With feathers in her mouth from the down inside his pant leg, she retraced her steps with aged grace. The man grabbed his ankle and threatened me and my animals with bodily harm. The other dogs were in a new attack formation, so I gave them orders to follow me and took off down the arroyo.

It was cowardly to run off without even inquiring if he was badly injured, but I'd seen them once before when they were keen on drawing blood. Once one had made the move, the others lashed about with their jaws open, tearing at anything including themselves. What I couldn't fathom, however, was why the attacker had been Burke, the oldest of the bunch. In her earlier career she had bitten at people indiscriminately, myself included. By accident, perhaps, she had once given me a nasty bite on the knee as I came up the hill and surprised her from sleep, but that had been a long time ago when she was only three or four years old. This had been a conscious attack, if I had ever seen one. The pathetic old hag with the fewest teeth had gone for blood and gotten duck's down. Lorry wouldn't believe it.

When I got back to the house, I told her the whole story. The dogs had arrived before I did, begging to be let inside. Sally, the coonhound, the dog most capable of slashing violence in a fight with other dogs, was crouched wide-eyed in a corner. I gave her a hug, and she rolled on her back and gave me love bites and sloppy licks—very unusual behavior for her.

"Must have been the smell. Did you say that the man had a peculiar smell on him?"

"He smelled bad of burned rubber, but that was from the tires. No, he had another smell, too, a chemical smell."

"You said ammonia before."

"It was like it, but it was different."

"Smell Sally's fur," Lorry said. "It smells really strange."

I got down on my knees and gave her fur a good whiff. It was the smell of the man. Wait a minute, I recognized it. When you kill ants, not with Raid, but by . . .

"Lorry," I almost shouted, "that smell's tannic acid, what ants have in their bodies. You know how it stinks when you've crushed an ant between your fingers." We were always killing ants in our house. Since most of it was buried beneath the ground, they tunneled through the adobe bricks and up into the flooring.

"Come to think of it, the smell of tannic acid was also on that cow's head today. It was tannic acid, I'm sure."

"Come to bed," Lorry said. "Let's turn out the lights. I don't want our house all lit up."

Completely drained, we crawled into bed. In the middle of the night, Lorry shook me awake to hear the chop-chop of a helicopter beat over the house and dust up the arroyo. The dog hullabaloo started all over again. All I could think before falling back asleep was that I hoped they all had shin guards.

Part Two
The Wound

7

Call my boss omniscient, intuitive, tyrannically correct in assumption after assumption, or just plain insidious, an event could not take place even in a staff member's head without Jamie Atkins's intimate knowledge. So I went to the office Monday morning expecting the worst. Jamie must know about my bullshitting at La Vida Friday night, and he probably knew even more than I did about the repercussions of Saturday afternoon. My only uncertainty was whether the occurrence Sunday night had disclosed itself to him through whatever means he employed to extract truth from the stars. But I had prepared and was ready for him.

"Alright," he said as I walked into my office. "Let's have it, your side of it, anyway."

"Friday night . . ."

"Not interested in Friday night."

His black eyes gleamed early morning intelligence. He would

enjoy every minute of this confrontation with me and the truth. I would not.

"I want to know what you have been doing on company time to unearth facts that would presumably lead to the premise that an article or series of articles might, one day soon, appear in bold print in our publication. That is what I want to know and nothing else."

"You're asking for a big order."

"Have you established any point of view that might give you an edge on any of the other reporters?"

"What other reporters? I thought I was alone in this pursuit."

"Don't be naive, Gerry. How do you think newspapers stay in print? The *Rio Grande Sun* is on it, as is the *New Mexican* and the *Reporter*. All of them have full-time correspondants greasing their wheels with activity. Are you aware of the latest developments with the FBI in our precinct here in Santa Fe? Have you followed the Salisbury affair or the Kreuger lead that appeared in Sunday's *New Mexican*? Have you picked up on any of the national releases on occult activities in Texas? Just what have you been doing since I gave you your assignment?"

Before words came to mind, I saw a kaleidoscope of the hopeless clues of my incipient search: a ruby beam intersecting a star, a big white dog with folded paws, a man in a silver suit.

"I'm waiting," he said, the skin on his forehead tight as a drum, his eyes out of joint, his lips put on wrong. The silence between us was a gas leak waiting for a match.

"I don't know," I groped. "I just don't know where I stand. My leads haven't been panning out."

"Wrong leads," he said with a whip in his voice. "You have to have some kind of premise. Nothing will land in your lap if you go out looking for anything at all. Do you agree?"

"I suppose so. The fact of the matter is that things have been happening too quickly for me to sort them out. I don't know what they mean yet."

"For instance?"

"I have already seen what may have been a mutilation, or it

could have been the work of a predator. I have also seen from very close up a human mutilation, that is, one effected by human means."

"Aren't they all?"

"At this point, I don't know."

"Are you in favor of some of the theories about aliens?"

"I don't know."

"Let's explore what you have said so far. Exactly what mutilation evidence have you laid eyes on, and what was its significance?"

"I saw a steer at the Pojoaque Dump that may have been mutilated by feral dogs."

"Have you delved into this incident any deeper than merely being aware of it? What I mean is, have you examined official reports to see if there is any evidence supporting a feral dog theory?"

"Predator theories are the authorities' favorites."

"I am aware of that. But have you checked into d-o-g-s?"

"Not yet."

"Finally we're getting somewhere. And the other incident you spoke of?"

"On Saturday, I saw a mutilated steer or heifer head, evidence of state policeman Angel Gomez. You've read about him, I'm sure. He was with Len Kreuger, that retired FBI guy. The head had been mutilated by some lunatic."

"Did the head look anything like this?" He held up a newspaper with a large photograph. Gomez and Kreuger were standing beside the head, as if they were the proud fathers.

"This came out Sunday in the *Rio Grande Sun.* Badly written piece, but somewhat informative. You could have done better. Let me just tell you one thing: try to stay away from the outlandish theories for awhile. You'll get nowhere running over to Los Alamos looking at laser beams. That's not the kind of story we want anyway—we want information that is immediately available. The science fiction can come later. Right now this is a political issue. Do you follow?"

"The lasers interested me for just that reason."

"They interest me, too. But you're not to fool around with Los Alamos. The University of California, their parent organization, has been confronting them lately as a result of Governor Brown hollering about money poured into weaponry projects that are top secret and do the public no ostensible good. See what I mean about politics? Sooner or later we all come down to the unpoetical broil of political issues. But what I'm trying to get across is that Los Alamos at the present time is off limits. I have information from a confidential source that if you had been a bit more indiscreet on Saturday, we might have been pressured with a lawsuit. Gerry, we just don't have time for anything that volatile right now. Besides, it is a dead end. Los Alamos is not conspiring to mutilate cattle."

"Maybe not directly, but did you ever consider that our government itself may be involved? Los Alamos has resources we know nothing about."

"I understand you know something about them. Well, be that as it may, I'm telling you to lay off Los Alamos. The main reason is that no one is talking over there and no one will talk over there. Scientists who break their oath of secrecy commit suicide."

"All reasons for my interest."

"Dammit, this is not Watergate, and I'm not going to have my building closed down because of defamation from your poking around in the sci-fi tubes over at Los Alamos.

"Now, this is what I want you to get for me. The *Sun* says a great amount of factual material concerning occult activity is presently available. Kreuger is willing to be interviewed at the present time because he's pushing to get instated as statewide investigator for the FBI. Gomez can't be trusted very far, but he is up to his ears in the thing, so you'd better interview him, too. What I want for our paper are clear-cut, factual, opinionated, down-to-earth interviews from people who are willing, ready, and able to give their views. There are state veterinarians with evidence, D.A.'s with the same, police records and files on occult activity, in short, endless sources for direct news. I want a story out next week. It doesn't have to be earth shattering, but it should be grounded in fact. At least it should be coming from the mouth of a living being who has something to do with the mutilations firsthand. Leave scientists, philosophers, poets, crackpots, and other credible or incredible wise guys and wise men for later. Understand your job?"

"Yes. One step at a time, with a report by next week."

"This week would be better. The other papers are making a lot of noise. And, by the way, Gerry, please read the other papers yourself. You should have had a lead on that Sunday 'head story.'"

"Unless I'm misinformed, we don't print a Sunday edition."

"You're misinformed. If the story's good enough, we may just put out a special issue on mutes."

"You seem to be up on the mute phenomena. What do *you* think is going on?"

"You want my own personal theory? Well, I don't have one. I found, however, an item in yesterday's paper quite intriguing. Let me read it to you: '. . . some criminologists have been saying that there is the possibility that contraband drugs are being injected into living cattle and later retrieved by means of surgically removing certain organs.' "

"How do these guys identify the cattle they've injected and how do they come and go without ever being seen?"

"Well, conjecture runs rampant, but some claim that the cattle are marked with a chemical dust that shows up at night under a certain kind of spotlight. The animals could be identified by helicopter, picked up, operated on in the air, and dropped. This theory undertakes to explain why many of the mutes are found with mashed necks and backs."

"What about the oil companies testing soil by dissecting cattle?"

"That's the environmental theory—giant corporations with megabucks looking for undiscovered fuel or mineral deposits. Some desert plants and grasses have root structures thirty to forty feet deep. Cattle eat surface material and become filter systems for their environment. Then along comes Mobil Oil, let us say, and uses these cattle as a barometer for well drilling operations. It may sound farfetched, but it is one popular opinion voiced in the *New Mexican* by Robert Grundig, just one week ago."

"The son of a bitch said he was covering some political thing."

"Down we come to the unpoetic broil of politics. You've got to have a handle to get reasonable results, Gerry. Sure, you can go at it the way you've been doing, hoping you'll hit your mark, but it's not practical. We can't afford it even if it were."

"Two theories are giving me the most trouble."

"Which ones?"

"One is the predator one. Most of the interviews I've read quote police officials or state employees as saying they believe the mute problem is related to predators. I have a real hard time believing that coyotes, wolves, mountain lions, vultures, owls, or eagles have any connection with cattle mutilations. What coyote or buzzard ever cored the rectal area or sexual organ of a dead animal? The surgery involved is too precise for a beak or a fang, anyway."

"I tend to agree with you. However, before you can the theory, I think you ought to hear it voiced in the first person."

"I'll check it out. The other theory I find unbelievable but nonetheless fascinating is the space theory."

"I won't give that theory credibility until someone comes face to face with a flying saucer that sucked up a cow—and is willing to swear testimony."

"So, now that we've ascertained that I've been wasting my time, where do you want me to begin?"

"Let's just say you've made a few detours. Why not interview someone who can support the cultist theory? That wouldn't be a bad start, and we could hustle something into print if you dig up somebody interesting.

"I may have an idea for you already. A friend of a friend of mine is writing a book about Taos in the old days.

"From what I've heard, he lambastes Taos in his book for allowing so many weird characters to hang around, you know, the

64

hippies leftover from the sixties. Did you know there was even a band of Druids living up there for a while?

"If you can link Druids with mutilated cattle all the power to you. I do remember something about them not too long ago, so it might be a fresh start. At least, there is a tangential story—that some pretty violent types who happen to have a lot of money have settled in Taos from time to time. You could get some good mileage out of that idea as long as you don't go too far astray. It might give you some other leads as well. Go for it—and don't waste any more time on laser beams or we'll all be selling postcards on the plaza."

8

Taos looks more like a mud-hut version of New England than New Mexico with its green-gold meadows and luxuriant leaf trees, but its refusal to change shows it belongs in spirit to the Southwest. It is the stronghold of a counterculture that persisted after the sixties and performed its own dance despite the death of radicalism.

For the old-timers who have lived in Taos since the days of D. H. Lawrence and company—when hitching rails was more in vogue than Model T's and it took a good day to travel by car the seventy miles that separate Santa Fe from Taos—the coming of the sixties' hippies of Haight-Ashbury was a bad dream.

The man I was going to interview, Bart Cross, had seen about as much of Taos in the halcyon days of the twenties as any living person. It was the changeover from those days to the present that

intrigued me. More particularly, how might the change in faces—
from old western Tom Mix hats and bandannas to beard, braid, and
dirt, as un-Indian as it was unpoetic—have helped create the violence that had erupted in recent years.

The hippies of the sixties had lived in tepees on the sage plains
on the other side of the great Rio Grande Gorge. They pretended to
be Anglo-Indian, but were, at least, washed, communally active, and
alert to the responsibilities of parenthood if only because it was "in."
Choirs of blonde beautiful people and their cherubs were seen
kissing one another in supermarkets. Now sullen, swollen types,
unkempt and uncaring, moved around in ones and twos.

Even so, going to Taos was always a day for dreaming. North of
town lay oceanic piles of golden hay in late summer or the waist-deep
furrows of wind-rushed grass in early spring. Taos Mountain, old
ground-down molar, rose out of nowhere and nothing, piney at the
gums and bare rock at the summit. Miles of reassuring sage were
unbroken except by an occasional adobe house.

Bart Cross met me at the door of his split-level house, which
had the low-slung look of a California redwood home except that the
outside was plastered. He was small with a thatch of snowy hair, and
dressed like the Taos artists of the thirties who had worn fat, knotted
ties and pressed, colored cotton shirts.

"I bought all those extra acres over that way, so I would have an
unbroken view of the mountains," he told me, "but look what they've
gone and done—built that damn tennis ranch over there."

He took me by the arm and led me inside to where his wife was
sitting by a big oak table. She was wearing an old-fashioned, blue
print dress which accentuated her straight-backed, resolute frame.
Here was a woman who had, like her husband and the land itself,
resisted every effort to go modern.

"This is Mrs. Cross," Bart said simply, and she rose and gave my
hand a hard shake.

"I think we'll be more comfortable in the studio," he said. "The
light in there is conducive to talk."

The studio was hers, and it was full of paintings and etchings, copper etching plates, and a large worktable covered with sketches. Mrs. Cross was one of America's maverick painters. Receiving the world's honors without so much as a smile or thank you, she always slipped back to her world of canyons and pueblo dancers.

"Well," Bart began, looking down at his feet, "a friend once asked me how it felt to be married to the world's greatest etcher and I asked him how he thought she felt being married to the world's worst poet." Both of them laughed like crazy while I stood there wondering what my response was supposed to be.

"Neither statement's accurate," he said at last. "We both do what we do, that's all."

"I wonder how much change you have seen up here since the early days."

"A good bit," he said.

"Heavens," she said.

"Were you here when Lawrence was in Taos?"

"Well, you mean," Bart said, "was Lawrence here when we were here, and the answer's yes. We didn't see much of him, not because we didn't like him, but because we didn't come to Taos in 1920 to see people. We came to get away from them."

"I guess the days of escape from people are pretty much over now," I said.

"That's the truth," Bart said. "Houses are popping up fast."

"We can still see Taos Mountain," she said, "and that's all we care about."

"You know there was a Taoseno here helping with our plastering not long ago, and my wife saw him looking rather wistfully up at those peaks over there. She said to him, quite matter of factly: 'We've been there.'

"He looked at her like, well, like she was stark raving mad, because what would a seventy-five-year-old white woman be doing up there on top of Taos Mountain? Then he said, 'What you see on top?' She replied calmly that at the top of the mountain was a broad flat expanse of nice clean grass. He smiled and went back to work and I heard him say to one of his friends, 'She been there alright.' "

"What's the strangest thing you ever saw in Taos?"

"The strangest thing? Let me see . . ."

"I can tell you the strangest thing I ever saw," Mrs. Cross said.

"What was it?" Bart asked, interested.

"The time you killed forty-eight rattlesnakes in a day."

"Oh that was way back when . . . you killed a lot of them when it got hot. The snakes always came out to drink at the irrigation ditches, so you'd get a good lick at 'em with a shovel. Mrs. Cross just layed that shovel on 'em, but not hard enough to hurt 'em at all, so I'd come over and give what-for, chop the head right off, then lay the limp body alongside my fence. Well, one day a Taoseno friend saw all those rattlers laid out in a row and he got to worrying. You know the Indians think differently than we do when it comes to snakes. He came right out and told me I was to learn to live with snakes."

"How easy has it been to learn to live with hippies?"

Mrs. Cross looked at her husband apprehensively and then said before he could answer:

"Nobody lives with the hippies but themselves. They're ignored in Taos."

"They weren't always ignored," he said. "There was a time when you couldn't walk the streets there were so many of them. We moved back to California when it got that bad, back in '69, I believe."

"Oh, those were awful times," she said. "Babies born out in the bushes with no one to care for them."

"What bothered me most of all was the game poaching," Bart said. "We have always respected nature and taken from her just what we needed to live. We have learned our ways from the Taos Indians. This hippie poaching problem was a real mess."

"I remember reading about an incident in Mora, an ingrown little New Mexican town if there ever was one. There must have been a couple of communes there at that time, around '69 or '70, and a hippie was shot and hung on a fence just like a coyote. The police wouldn't do a thing about it."

68

"That is precisely the atmosphere I am talking about. Perfectly innocent people were killed because of the rudeness of their friends."

"Let's not talk about it, dear," Mrs. Cross said. "Let's be thankful that it has passed."

"But it hasn't," he said adamantly. "Now there's the mutilation thing going on. I have said all along it's hippies poaching cattle this time instead of deer."

"They are using some pretty sophisticated equipment," I said. "Some say it's government work."

"Nonsense. Look at that Druid affair a year ago; they were a breed of hippie. Don't get me wrong, I know all about the original Druids. The Greek word for oak was *drus*, and they were called oak priests because they did their rituals under oak trees in Great Britain. Yeats himself said he was a Druid."

"These new Druids, what were they?"

"Hippies. They were a bunch of half-starved and half-crazy kids with some little bits of misinformation about Druidry rattling around in their heads. Nobody knows much about the original Druids because they are a part of our mythology. They may have been perfectly peaceable folk. Who knows whether they made sacrifices of children, as they were later described as doing, or let the blood of a lamb flow into a stone cup just as the sun came up or set. Nobody knows. But these kids up on the Navajo reservation near Rama— that's the part of the Navajo tribe that even the Navajos don't want to associate with—were cutting off dogs' heads and drinking blood and all manner of idiocy until they were finally caught at it and put in jail."

"Were they sentenced for animal cruelty?"

"No. They were thrown in jail for killing an infant. Sacrificing it to their god."

"We don't know the particulars, dear," Mrs. Cross said, "just what we read in the papers."

"What makes you think the hippies are responsible for killing cattle and cutting them up?" I said.

"If those Druid kids could kill a baby and drink its blood, then our own Taos hippies could certainly take it upon themselves to cut up cows."

"Come with me," Bart said rising from his chair. "I want you to see something."

We walked to the side of the house. There was a tool shed and a well cap, and nearby he had arranged a collection of stones like a Japanese garden. They were laid out in circles and rows according to size, color, and shape. He bent down and took a bunch of small, black flint chips.

"I want you to have these," he said fatherly.

Up close, I saw that they weren't flints at all.

"The Spanish call these black crystals *lagrimas de Cristo*. You can find them buried up in the hills where the Ponderosas start. I used to go up there all the time; all we did was hike in the old days. I want you to keep these in your pocket for good luck."

I held out my hand and he put a goodly number of the little stones in it.

"Each one of these is a cross!"

"Yes," he said, "a perfect cross. Hard to believe nature could chisel anything just like a sculptor's hand. Keep 'em to remember me by. We've got the same last name, so you've got a little piece of Cross to protect you."

I was moved by his kind gesture and the beauty of the crystals. The sky overwhelmed us with its purple glow.

"Right over there is where the watchers would be," he said, pointing to a pyramid-shaped mountain on the horizon toward Santa Fe.

"The watchers?"

"Taosenos. At this time of day they'd be looking for Navajo raiding parties. The Pueblos were a peaceful people, but they could fight like hell if they had to. The Spanish learned that the hard way. I can see the watchers sitting cross-legged in the gathering dusk, keeping an eye out for any evil stalking the plains."

70

9

To what did the Druids praying on the red sands outside of Rama pray—clouds, sandstone cliffs, ravens? Surely not to the stunted oaks. It was difficult to relate them to those hooded figures who kneeled under massive Irish oaks three hundred years old. These kids were different Druids, and they demanded more from me than the casual questioning of Bart Cross.

At the county courthouse in Santa Fe, I unearthed the records of the trial in which the Druidic band had been charged with the murder of a six-month-old infant. Until that time they had been allowed to camp and live where they pleased, though their base camp was outside Rama. Santa Fe, with its soil blessed by ancient rites, curses, and miracles, attracted them for several months every year. They traveled in an old school bus decorated with gypsy symbols. The little hexes and crosses had told dark-eyed wanderers of Rumania more than a hundred years ago where to find shelter or food, where the weather was bad or the people inhospitable, where the mountains were uncrossable, where a bridge was washed out or rebuilt.

The bus would be seen parked under a copse of cottonwoods on Tesuque Pueblo land next to a fenced-in water tank. The Druids sat and stared at the Indian cattle that roamed freely all around the watered, willowy countryside surrounding the tank. Then the bus would be gone. Its ragged, bearded passengers would leave nothing behind except a pair of coveralls hanging from a low limb of one of the great cottonwoods. The Indians parked their pickups under the shade of those trees and stuck copious numbers of beer cans in the pockets of the coveralls and a bottle into the open fly. This scarecrow hung on in memory of the vanished band.

It was after one of the vigils at the end of a long hot summer that a pueblo Indian fishing by the lake discovered a small burial mound. Underneath was the slug-shaped form of a fetal-crouched infant of about six months.

The trial that followed the capture of the band—six adults, male and female, and several half-grown children—proved only that they had been camping near the lake shortly before the dead child was discovered.

There were no witnesses to swear that the Druids had had a child of the buried one's age in their company. Bored with the proceedings of several weeks of questions that got nowhere, a Santa Fe judge banished the bunch from the state of New Mexico. They resettled in Australia.

The autopsy of the baby showed that it had died of influenza. The only conclusive facts known about its short, faded life were that it had been born, had lived six months in the probable uncare of some parent or nonparent, and had died and been buried by an Indian lake.

The pueblo reaction was that signs went up everywhere where no signs had been before. Several pueblos instigated laws saying that non-Indians would have to get special permission in writing from the governor of the pueblo to pass through Indian land. Members of the Spanish and Anglo community are still battling these laws in the courts today, saying that if certain access routes were cut off, they would be forced to drive up to a hundred miles out of their way to get to work every day.

Then in the court records I found a part of the Druid saga that really interested me: a year ago, a couple and their son had defected from the ranks in the outback of Australia and come back to Santa Fe. Starting in Miami, they had traveled leisurely across the country in a microbus which was later discovered broken down in the burned-out, mined-out hills south of Cerrillos, twenty miles outside Santa Fe. They had been tried for stealing, and during their trial many rumors had connected them to the cattle mutilations. I decided to locate someone who knew something about the two Druids who had returned to Santa Fe soil.

Tom Ahern was a fiddler who had come to Santa Fe from the

San Francisco Chronicle. He had quit newspapering except when circumstances drove him to knock out a quick two thousand-word piece for one of the two decent papers in town. It was through his coverage of the Druid return that I was able to find him, living in a beat up trailer in Cerrillos.

He, his wife, and his adopted Navajo son lived in the trailer. His writing, fiddling, painting studio was a cave in a boulder-strewn hillock. Passing through a shaft of gauzy salt cedars, you entered into a world set apart from the Cerrillos sun. The inside walls were rough-plastered cement decorated with pictograms. The troll inhabitant, Tom, was putting a new string on his fiddle as I came inside.

For awhile I forgot all about my assignment and drank in the dark coolness. Tom, who had been phoned of my arrival (the cave had a phone, a water spigot, and a fireplace made of natural stone with a hole for a flue) ignored me as he restrung his little heart-shaped fiddle. His son sat beside him, the quietude of his Navajo moonface completely Oriental: he was aware of no other moving or living thing but his father.

Tom was a big bear of a man but as he tuned up, I saw that his large fingers moved like hummingbirds. The high trills were like the honeysuckle vines that hung down the smoke hole above the crude red stone fireplace.

"What'd you wanna know?" he grumbled after a few minutes of idle trilling.

"That was fine fiddling," I said.

The whites of his eyes shone in the blue shade of the grotto. He looked enchanted with my comment.

"Wish I could make a living with this thing. What'd you come for—that Druid thing?"

"I work for the *New Mexico Review*. I have to do a feature on the cattle mutilations, and that's how I got into the Druid trial."

"They killed cows," he said cryptically.

"I haven't been able to dig up much on it."

"That's because there's nothing to dig, and I won't add to the smear that's already in print. My article was bad enough."

"You knew them, didn't you?"

73

"The boy was a little retarded, but they took care of him okay."

"Did they ever speak to you about killing cattle?"

"That was in the papers. I didn't write it."

"As far as the cattle mutilation thing goes . . ."

"Look, I don't mean to be rude because I know you are just doing a job, like I do when I have to. Those people were alright. They just happened to have a far-out religion. If they killed a cow or two, that was between them and the rancher that caught them. To tell you the truth, I don't know any more about it than you do. All I know is they stole some stuff, a saddle I think it was, to pay for some food. Because they were who they were they got the book thrown at them. There were all kinds of rumors linking the cattle mutilations to them. Personally, I think that was just scapegoating."

"Their being in jail hasn't prevented mutilations, has it?"

"Nope."

"You knew the husband pretty well, I heard. What was he like?"

"Like you or me, only poorer. He didn't seem to have any horse sense. They were both incapable of earning a living."

"Why did they return to Santa Fe?"

"Incapability to do anything right. They could have stayed in Australia the rest of their lives, but they wandered back without any real reason except they were tired of it over there, and they liked Santa Fe better than any place they'd ever lived."

"Your interview described some pretty hard times."

"Yeah. They liked to lie around on the rocks doing whatever it was they liked to do—talk to God, I guess. When winter socked in all of a sudden, you remember those October snows, they just holed up in Madrid. They moved from one deserted mine shack to another, bumming food and huddling in the cold, wrapped up in sacks. Around the time I first met them they were staying in a shack with no windows, so they put some cracked tar paper over window frames, banged nails in place with a rock, and sat in front of an old coal stove that had been abandoned in 1933. The place was so smoky it made you cough just to stand at the door."

"What happened after the saddle incident?"

"You probably know as much as I do about that. They were starving, even though a bunch of us were feeding them with anything we had to give, so they busted into the Woolcott Ranch tack room. Nobody was there except a night watchman who was asleep at the time. They stole a saddle and tried to sell it down the road to a rancher for a couple hundred bucks. They were caught right away. Then because they were Druids, all this other stuff was heaped on them, and now they are put away and our civilization's safe again."

"What happened to the kid?"

"Ward of the state. Partly retarded, remember."

"Well, now they can't hurt themselves, anyway, or that boy. He'll probably get better care from the state."

"You think so?"

As I walked down the road that led back to the trailer and the dusty lot where I had parked my car, I heard sweet strains of fiddle tangling in the blue air, wailing like the nasal droning of the unforgettable song of the Penitentes.

10

By Thursday of the third week into the mute probe, I had enough material to write the first in the projected series of essay interviews entitled: "The Manic Panic of Mutology," in which I would focus on the relationship between mutology and the other violent events of our lives which we have come to think of as normal.

"What," I asked in my best rhetoric, "makes the mute phenomena abnormal? What makes it phenomena at all?" The

Druid affair and the rape and murder of an old lady living alone in Santa Fe had aroused much less attention in the community. Why the fuss over the mutes? The answer I offered, perhaps naively, was that we humans are always ready for the great event that explains all the others. "Are we the creators of the mute mystery, are we ourselves, even as observers, the phantom surgeons?" I asked cryptically.

Within one hour of the appearance of my front-page story, the phone at the *Review* began to jump. I was unprepared for the tidal wave of disgust.

"I'm a cattle rancher in Springer," drawled a voice with all the warp of wind on the plain and leather left to linger in the sun, "and you're so full of shit it's coming out your boot tops!" He hung up. Hate calls allow no rebuttals. They kept coming in, and I kept taking them one after another like bitter tonic, which after the first draft is no longer poison.

A cult member called me a "shit-faced hypocrite" and added that it was people like myself that inspired the manic panic by writing drivel that bent innocent minds.

"I know where you get that stuff. Who knows what evil lurks in the hearts of men? You're just an old fan of the Shadow, just like me, tee, hee." Obviously, an old prospector thirsty for a laugh since his mule died.

I was mad at myself for not predicting the response my hypnotic prose would have in a town that was still three-quarters cowboy and Indian.

Jamie Atkins found the episode amusing.

"I think you've got their dander up," he said pouring himself a hefty mug of coffee. "Frankly, I'm surprised. At them and you. What did you mean by all that talk about 'We are the creators' and so on. You didn't mean any of it literally, of course. You have hit on a rather interesting psychological tension spot, but you failed to nail anything down. Are these events interior or exterior, answer me that."

"I don't know what you mean, interior or exterior," I said. "The whole point I was trying to make—stupidly from the response we're getting—is that all these things are related by violence."

"I'll go along with that, even if they do not, but what I am trying to pull out of you is whether or not you believe these things you call mutilations are happening at all."

"Goddamn right they're happening. We all know that. You don't think I'm that stupid, do you?"

"I don't think you're stupid at all. I think you're miles ahead of your reading audience. That's what the fuss is all about. I'm very pleased with what you have set in motion. Get angry, write another what's happening out here folks article, but next time I want you to do me a favor. Don't tell us what we already know or suspect or are afraid is true. Tell us what you think you see."

"I already did that."

"What you did was tell us right off the bat what you *thought*. Now tell us what you think you *see*. If you don't know for sure, tell us anyway. Scare us sick with the sight of that rawhided bloody bone."

"Why don't you ever back us up? You give us these damn idiotic assignments, then you're never satisfied. You always press for more. You squeeze us dry."

The heat rose in the room.

Jamie sat there at his three-cornered desk, his hands folded primly. Over the blue serge suit, I envisioned frilled gambler's cuffs and gold links.

"I'll back you and anyone else on my staff the moment you or he is in trouble. You have to trust me to know when that time comes. Right now, you're experiencing the calm before the storm."

His cold assurance rankled. He was just playacting, not at all involved. That was really my problem: against my will, again and again, I was getting involved with a story that I would rather have read about and thrown away.

"Define your varmint," he challenged. "Call it out and pin a tail on it, unless you don't think it'll stand for it."

"I want to go home for the day," I said.

"Permission granted." All seventy of his teeth were shining at my defeat.

Marsha, our receptionist, poked her head in the open doorway. "Sorry, Ger, someone on line three wants a word with you. Should I say you're out for the day?"

"I'll take it."

"Good boy," Jamie said approvingly.

"Hot dog," the phone voice intoned, "you did well. So well, in fact, that you protected practically everyone from knowing anything. Very stylish."

I knew the voice, but I couldn't identify it.

"Who is this?"

"Me. You'll be getting a call next week from someone I've given your article to. You might even get a confession. Who knows?" The voice clicked off.

"That was impolite," Jamie said from the next room. He had been listening on his extension, one of his operative tactics that no longer daunted me. "Who do you think that was?" he asked without getting up from his chair.

"Someone I know but can't quite place."

"Gravelly old Grundig from the *New Mexican*."

"What do you think his asinine message meant?"

"He was killing you with kindness. Now he'll throw a carcass at your feet, just watch."

"My eyes are wide open," I said and went out the door.

Lorry assured me that what I had written had made good sound sense and was ahead of its time, just what I needed to hear and what she knew I needed to hear. The alchemy of deep sleep put me back on track. I was out for a good time in the house of horrors once more and I was not going to be tricked again.

I decided to review the entire subject of mutilations. A fearsome number of mutilations were recurring on Indian reservations nationwide, but in greater concentration in the Southwest. A great percentage was on big western ranches with a smaller frequency on small midwestern or eastern farms. Almost no mutilations had occurred on national forest lands. A formidable group of mutologists was claiming that the majority of mutes happened near nuclear facilities. Meticulously researched maps showed this relationship with exact mileages. The people who drew such maps also perceived lines of demarcation between "them," the military-megacorporate-government-aliens, and "us," the helpless, innocent Americans. I didn't put much faith in maps and mapmakers.

I really felt the Druids, Sikhs, and other weird religious orders were incapable of executing a massive mutilation offensive. Nor did any of the groups seem interested in that end; they were too focussed on themselves. True, they were committed to their own delicacies of ornate belief, like the group that drank a glass of their own piss each morning. The Sikhs seemed to be an inhospitable clan involved in religion as an effortless way to make money. The Druids were sadists, bloodletters, bestialists, but too aimless to undertake a vast enterprise of ritual slaughter. I was all for chucking the connection and going for something deeper—a more native form of mystical behavior, perhaps.

Many people saw a possible source of violence in the eternal conflicts between Anglos and Indians. Unfortunately, neither side would talk openly. The most I had been able to get out of an Indian friend of mine from Santa Clara Pueblo, speaking strictly off the record, was that the mutilations were a form of evil not solely propagated by whites, but that they could not be ruled out either. Primary suspects in his mind were the nearby religious orders and, highest in his personal favor, other Indians. He explained the latter by saying intermarriages between pueblos had so diluted the family clans and religious orders that conflicts had arisen between families that had once been inseparable.

What he told me was in line with my own thinking: something broken needed mending. I thought of the dances of the plains tribes to bring back the buffalo. Was it time again to cleanse an old wound, with the mutes an Indian healing ritual? Or were the mutilations the wound itself, an Indian trauma in the making?

Suddenly the phone startled me out of my reverie. The moment

I heard the voice, I knew it was my mystery caller.

"What's new at the *Review*? Hey, that rhymes, doesn't it? Maybe I should get out of the ad business and take up poetry."

I recognized the biggest, old ad man in Santa Fe, who never recognized you on the street unless you were about to introduce him to somebody famous or serve him a summons. Art Coffin was a crew-cut character who somehow made you believe that he was as good as gold, no matter how indecent his proposal. He would be guest of honor at the Elk's Club fund-raising dinner, yet when the Citizens for Native Americans had their yearly powwow he would come out smiling in favor of giving Santa Fe back to the Indians.

He was an American go-getter who knew that rules were only made to be broken. But now, he was being sued. Public opinion had him up against an adobe wall and he was looking for a crack in the plaster to crawl into.

"Listen," Coffin told me, "I know what some of you guys think about Mountains West. How's about giving me a turn. I think that's only fair."

"I guess we owe you that, only I'm on another assignment right now. It doesn't matter to me what happens in the courts. I just hope the Indians get their six million dollar check for reparations."

"You guys kill me. You don't care about people, just causes. A lot of guys are getting fried on fake accusations and you tell me you're rooting for the Indians. Don't you forget that we're the ones who pay for the lousy advertising in your cheap little review."

"We appreciate the support."

"Those Indians don't buy ads, do they? We do, the guys in the hot seat, who didn't do anything but make Santa Fe a healthier place to live until all this fuss got blown up in the papers. Well, I have something to say, if you have a mind to listen. I'll set you straight and leave you to draw your own conclusions. What d'you say?"

"I'm game, Mr. Coffin. But remember, I'm not on assignment. I can't do a thing for you."

"What assignment are you on anyway? What could be more newsworthy than Mountains West?"

"I'm doing the cattle mutilations."

"Well, I'll be dipped in shit for a doughnut. Alright, meet me at the Green Onion in forty-five minutes and I'll wrap that up for you, too. Nobody knows more cowboys in this damn town than I do."

"The cowboys aren't killing their own cattle."

"All depends on what you consider a cowboy, my man. Those guys with feathers in their hair wear cowboy hats, too. Green Onion in forty-five minutes."

I pulled a folder marked Mountains West Development Corporation out of the bottom drawer of my desk. The file dated back to October 1972, the month the rats were caught in their own trap. I read the now-famous ad prepared by the Coffin Association:

> Live in peace and tranquility in your own custom-built solar home at the base of the Sangre De Cristo Mountains in the foothills of the Rockies.
>
> Here, in the Golden West, you will find luxury you can afford, elegance without expense.
>
> Golf course, abundant water supply, gently rolling hills.
>
> Seclusion you always dreamed about.
>
> Each home custom made for comfort and only 11 minutes from the Plaza of America's second oldest city.

It was copy that couldn't fail, and didn't until a few illegalities and under-the-carpet ignominies turned up. I glanced at one of the headlines we had run at the *Review:* MOUNTAINS WEST: THE BIGGEST LAND WAR SINCE THE 19TH CENTURY.

Another one read: POLITICAL RESIGNATIONS AND SU-PREME COURT RUMORS: HOWARD HUGHES AND THE MAFIA MEET AT MOUNTAINS WEST TO DISCUSS THE INDIAN PROBLEM.

Actually the plot was quite uncomplicated, at first anyway. A bunch of good old boys picked up an Indian land lease for ninety-nine years and were all set to turn five thousand acres of chamisa brush into astroturf when the pueblo old-timers put on their specs and read the fine print on their contract for the first time. That was the beginning of a six million dollar lawsuit. Indian pleas to the Bureau of Indian Affairs read: "You have not assisted us in our needs . . . It is odd that you refuse to give us good advice or even guarantee us a good lawyer. We have tried to get help from our guardian, and you have betrayed us."

One of the members of the Mountains West development team threw up his arms when he heard this. "We're up to our ass in Indians and I feel kind of like Custer."

A battle between the old and the young on both sides was finally brought out into the open when someone tossed a Molotov cocktail into the Mountains West Real Estate office one night. What remained of the mess was a Custer's Last Stand in the courts of New Mexico and a great pile of redwood siding, broken into bite-sized pieces for the warming of many pueblo hearths.

"The whole thing was one great jurisdictional battle," Coffin explained to me in a carefully modulated whisper over a Bloody Mary at the Onion. "Even now I don't think there is anything morally wrong with Mountains West Development Corporation."

I was unable to forget that the man seated before me had once been a state senator. His discomfort seemed to arise not from what he was going to tell me, but from the lack of a legitimate audience to tell it to.

"Everybody wants to be the last s.o.b. to move to Santa Fe," he went on. "That's why the county laws came down so hard on us. We had a ninety-nine year lease on the property across the road from the pueblo. The Indians had signed the lease over to us, and it was as legal as Columbus Day. Then the city council instructed the city attorney to obtain an injunction against us, on opening day no less. So we turned around and got a temporary restraining order against the city of Santa Fe prohibiting interference."

"How did you manage to pull that off?"

"We got a district judge who happened to be Senator Manuel's cousin to push it through."

"And then . . ."

"Well, you probably remember the city got a second district

82

judge to slap a second temporary restraining order which prohibited us from commencing sales. Next thing we knew the matter was before the Supreme Court. Do you know who made the ruling there?"

"I don't recall."

"Donald Steppenhouse, a former partner in the law firm that represented Tesuque Pueblo. He suspended the second district judge's temporary restraining order, and our grand opening was ready to proceed."

"Didn't the Indians claim their counsel was biased? Didn't the lawyer for Mountains West represent the Indians as well?"

Coffin held his Bloody Mary to his lips and licked the edge of his glass. His fat, pink fingers diminished the glass. His eyes rolled about the room at the few people lounging around in various attitudes of indifference. Coffin turned back to me and set his drink on the table.

"I don't like to admit to error," he said tightening his lips and frowning. "But if it has to be done, I'll be frank about it. To tell you the truth, that lawyer business was a grand farce. We did have a lawyer who also gave counsel to the pueblo."

"So you admit to making a mistake in covering up the basic corruption of selling homes that had no water supply, no police or fire protection, no sewage treatment plant, no school bus facility, and no vital utilities such as gas or electricity. Just think of a population of fifteen thousand in the middle of nowhere with no lifelines."

"Don't wax melodramatic."

"That's my job."

"Listen, young fellow. I'm not saying there weren't some loose bolts in the foundation. But my job was to promote a housing complex that would have brought hard cold cash to the Tesuque Pueblo and to the city of Santa Fe. We were told that since the subdivision was on Indian land, all non-Indian residents could expect the same immunities as the Indians themselves."

"I know for a fact that only a handful of Indians, the older members of the pueblo, were unaware of what was happening. The younger ones knew it spelled disaster just as the Indians at Sandia Pueblo knew that a dog track on their land was a basic evasion of state racing and liquor laws. Wasn't Howard Hughes himself pushing for the track down there, along with plans for a resort and a casino on Navajo land?"

"I think your attitude is very naive. Where do you think the money comes from that supports our life-style in New Mexico? Out-of-state dollars keep this bright land from going back to the horned toads. I say if Howard Hughes or anybody else wants to build or buy a parcel of Indian sagebrush, he should be able to do it for the betterment of all."

"Can I quote you on that?"

"No, you may not. I was hoping you would have an open mind, but I can see you've already put yourself on the opposite side of the fence. Well, I'm not surprised."

"I told you on the phone I wasn't really interested in Mountains West. My assignment is cattle mutilations. You don't have to worry about bad press coming from me."

Coffin stared into the bloodred rime in his glass. "That cattle business is directly related to Mountains West. And you and I both know who is responsible for that bombing."

"We do?"

"Don't play the dumb reporter. You're too smart for that. The realty office was blown up by the same protestors who drew up that petition against us, the group called Tewa Tesuque, those goddamn tomahawk heads did it. They also carted off every loose board on that property. There were plenty of witnesses who saw them load up their pickups with office stuff that didn't belong to them."

"It was on their land wasn't it?"

"None of it belonged to them. It was the property of the corporate owners of Mountains West. The Indians lifted it without so much as a thought."

"You were going to pump millions of gallons of their water without a thought so you could sprinkle a golf course. But I don't know what any of this has to do with cattle mutilations."

"Simple. The Indians are cutting up good beef the same way they blew up buildings that didn't belong to them."

"Cutting up their own cattle? To serve what purpose? Half of the animals I've seen mutilated were right on Indian land."

"Doesn't that make it all the more believable? They make it look like they're being victimized when actually they're the ones who are perpetrating the crime."

"Now all you have to do is explain how they suck cow's blood and leave without being seen or leaving any tracks."

"Don't ask me how witches do their thing. Ask them. They've been doing it for a thousand years."

11

I was not about to discount a much different connection between mutilations on Tesuque Indian land and the Mountains West land scam. The mutilations could be a scheme to scare pueblo leaders into auctioning off properties that they once mistakenly leased. The most effective way to undermine any unified group is through an attack on its spiritual and religious center of being. Certain cultural anthropologists had already suggested this explanation for mutilations near which helicopters or their skid marks had been seen.

Somewhere in this puzzle seemed to fit the elderly woman that some people insist tooled down the Taos Highway in a mint condition Model T just before the Mountains West real estate office was blown up. Her name was Sundee O'Grady, but everyone called her the Snake Lady because of her fondness for the five-foot slippery pets she took out dancing with her to bars and parties. At sixty, she would wear a Follies Bergere outfit with a red satin snake's head on the crotch, two rubber snakes braided into her hair and a real one in her handbag.

She was famous not only because she thought of herself as famous, but because during the Second World War she had been the only Allied female fighter pilot to accomplish successful missions over various war zones.

In more recent years, she had had a reputation for blowing up highway signs and other blights on the landscape. With an ancient love of explosives, she seemed to have a penchant for turning political schemes into piles of flying paper.

A day out of the office away from calls was worth staring at a bunch of snakes in an old lady's bosom. I drove out to see her on her sprawling adobe ranch house on the Arriba River outside Santa Fe.

What do you say on meeting a woman of seventy who looks forty, and who reaches down like an acrobat to scoop a handful of dog poop off the floor with her bare hand while explaining the acceptable method of freezing stillborn rabbits for snake food?

"I have every snake stool of this year calibrated and collected for future reference and use," she explained enthusiastically. "Did you know that when you feed a tinted Easter chick to a grown bull snake, the stool will come out pure pink? Beautiful, a real work of art."

She led me to the room off the kitchen where her darlings were housed in immense glass terrariums. Yellow and black heads rose inquisitively at the sound of her voice.

"There they are, my sweets. Look how they come to the sound of my voice, just like puppies." It was true. The snakes flickered and curled like mustard flames. Great loops of them uncoiled sinewy and slack, the eyes either beaded and sharp or cloudy.

"Those dearies with the misty eyes are shedding their old skins now. They can't see you, but their tongues can pick up who you are and what you're about probably better than any human."

"I'd enjoy holding one of them in my hand."

"Well, bless your heart. Let me fetch Herman the Hungry for you. He's a sleek one."

She reached into one of the glass cubicles and ten or more snakes lifted their heads and pressed themselves into her open palm. Serpents twined in rapture all about her palm and up her arm.

"Only Herman this time. Sorry Angela, dear. Donald Do-Bite, where are your manners?"

On command the unwanted reptiles slunk from her arm like whipped mongrels. She swept the one remaining snake to my face for a closer look.

"Here's my precious Herman," she said, her eyes sparkling. "Treat him as you would a baby. He won't hurt you."

"I like snakes," I told her, which was true.

I took a seat on a kitchen chair. The cool snake twined around my arm, scales rippling with muscled balance and agility. No smoother thing had ever been on my arm. I didn't mind its being there, nor did it seem undisposed to attach itself to me. This was not lost on the admiring glitter of my new friend Sundee.

"Didn't you mention there was something you wanted to ask me?"

Herman the Hungry directed his head toward the vibration of her voice. His little splinter of a tongue shot quickly in and out as he moved in slow motion.

"That's alright, Herman, dear," she whispered. "We're among friends. You can lie down now."

The bull snake flattened its three-foot length along my arm, returned its head to its tail, and pressed its hard, flat head deep into my skin.

"Oh, he likes you," she purred. "Do you know that a bull snake has two penises? I have a picture of them in action. Would you like to see it? They're called hemopenises, and I don't know why Herman has to have two of them, but I am sure they must double Angela's pleasure. She is pregnant, you know. What lovely spring eggs we're going to have. What was it you were going to ask me a moment ago?"

No preamble was necessary with this woman. I spoke as directly to her as she spoke to her snakes.

"Do you think there's any connection between the cattle mutilations and the Mountains West land deal?"

Her long silent look seemed to suddenly question whether I was friend or foe.

"What's this for?" she said sharply.

"For me," I said.

"Will this appear in print somewhere?"

"It could, depending on what you tell me."

"I don't want to be quoted. There are enough nasty rumors going around. Why, someone even spread word that *I* was the one who burned up that real estate office. Well, it *was* an offensive projection of the male ego, but I wouldn't blow it up on that account. Besides, the pueblo has already taken responsibility for it. Some angry Indian kids did it. But who can know for sure? Maybe one of the realtors . . . Coffin himself might have done it for the insurance."

"Hardly likely. An insurance claim couldn't have begun to cancel his debt. It's up in the millions."

"My snakes could learn M.O. from *that* man, but to call *him* a snake would be an insult to my Herman."

"I'm curious about the mutilation implications—someone getting even for past wrongs. Does that make any sense to you?"

"Everything makes sense if you look at it the right way. I deplore cattle; they're not nearly as intelligent as snakes. I also deplore people who cut up cattle for no good reason.

"The Indians don't make it any easier on themselves. At least once a week someone in Tesuque has to round up the pueblo cows after they've trampled a nice garden or destroyed a corn crop or something. Then the pueblo governor's incensed when one of the cows gets hit by a cowboy in a pickup truck. If they let them wander all over creation, what do they expect? But look at it this way: once upon a time *all* this land belonged to one or more of the many pueblos scattered about these hills. Did I tell you I found a child's skull, six hundred years old, teeth bright as diamonds, right out in my backyard?"

"Do you think Coffin or any of his cohorts would have reasons to harm the pueblo's cattle?"

"He'd do it for the fun of it, and it wouldn't cost him a penny."

"Why not?"

"Don't be naive. The man was a senator. He has connections like taproots all the way to New York. How do you think he pulled off Mountains West in the first place?"

"I don't believe he did. He was caught and now he'll pay the price."

"We'll see how he worms out of this one. Please observe, I would never say crawls out of this one. That would be treason, wouldn't it, Herman dear?" Herman poked his head out of the crook of my arm, tongue flashing messages.

"Come to Mama," she said, and the limp coil went toward her as bidden. He navigated the tabletop smoothly and made for Sundee's copious bosom. She sat motionless as he slid down the opening at the top of her throat and descended into the netherworld.

"Does he always do that?"

"He hides whenever he hears Coffin's name."

"I see."

"I'll tell you something you oughtn't repeat. If someone wants to hit the pueblos where they really live, they should have a go at their religion, because that's what's kept them together all these hundreds of years."

"How would one go about it? Witchcraft?"

"A good scare would work the best, but how would depend on what you were trying to accomplish. Fire works a magic on certain people, but now a cow missing its tongue is another kind of magic altogether."

"Do you know how to cast spells, Sundee?"

"Herman, where do you think you're going—and in front of company." She reached deep into her blouse and fetched Herman out by the tail. She reeled him in backwards.

"The only thing you don't want to do with a snake," she said, "is to get him into a place he doesn't want to come out of."

"That applies to rats, as well," I said.

"That applies to snakes going after rats," she said.

12

I parked in a public lot in downtown Albuquerque and headed for the library, where a calm sea of cowboy hats floated upon the small group of informally clothed men and women that leaned against the walls and windows of the building. The lines were distinctly drawn: mostly cowboys and cattlemen in large straws or small stetsons, some hatless Anglo and Spanish politicians, a uniformed officer here and there, and nervous newspeople swapping notes and exchanging cards. The atmosphere was like a party, but no one knew exactly what was going to be served.

Laughter was restrained. Shoulders shifted. Eyes moved from face to face, as if getting acquainted too soon was not proper. In this atmosphere of indecision I found myself suddenly shy. Then a straight-backed, mustached fellow came up to me. "Peter Argyle," he smiled. "Professor of applied cultural anthropology, University of Vancouver. You're a writer, aren't you?" he said. "You're holding your briefcase like you've only got one chapter left to go."

"Fact is I'm just sorting through the facts. Haven't put a word on paper yet."

"Good man. No need to draw any conclusions, especially when the facts are so hit or miss. Even calling them facts at all is a bit ludicrous at this point."

Hats and heads began turning toward the glass doors of the library. The two or three hundred people that had gathered began to eddy into the cool auditorium downstairs. A television crew was swarming over hotlights, rotary cameras, and myriad of wires and hookups. A long table was prepared at the left-hand corner of the stage, and a stenographer's chair and desk were just to its right.

Harrison Salisbury, New Mexico senator and former astronaut, entered from the wings with Brinton Shaw, the district attorney, who took a seat at the long table. The senator walked up to the podium for an opening line of welcome. Just as he got there a cameraman's lamp fell from a great height and smashed on the floor in front of the stage. Salisbury seized the incident for his opener.

"These days you have to keep a lookout for UFO's even inside public buildings," he said.

The audience laughed. The tension seemed to ease, and a few Indians even cracked smiles.

"We have, as you know," the senator began, "brought about this conference because of mounting public concern over the $2.5 million of property damage that has occurred in the past year as a result of cattle mutilations in our state. Now what's hard for me to accept is that, up until now, no federal crime was committed. It wasn't until last week that my colleague Wallace Smith, our newly assigned agent at the Department of Justice, who is with us today, discovered the two clauses that will allow us to launch a major investigation.

"It is terribly hard for me to accept that we actually had to search for a federal law that was being broken before we could get moving on this thing. What Wallace Smith has done for us is to find the legal loopholes, if you will, whereby we can finally act, and hopefully prosecute the perpetrators of these bizarre mutilations.

"In brief, the laws that have been broken are these: first and foremost, the illegal operating of unmarked and unregistered aircraft, and second, the deliberate assault of properties belonging to American Indians. Both of these fall under federal jurisdiction. So we hope today to reaffirm our goodwill with the pueblo leaders of northern New Mexico, as well as other tribal leaders, so that they may assist us in our efforts to bring cattle mutilations to a stop in our state.

"Before closing my statement and going on with our proceedings, I would like to say that what makes our predicament so untenable is the unprecedented discipline employed by these offenders. To my knowledge, there has not been a crime perpetrated in twenty-three states thus far in our history that leaves us with so few actual clues. This fact alone deserves our closest scrutiny and our best scientific approach. Thank you for coming here today and offering your collective support to our cause."

The first speaker of the day was Oliver Parsons, director of the Social Science program at Yale. He looked earnest and athletic. "I belong to a nationwide network of researchers who are trying to determine the exact nature of the mutilations. Let us say, for simplicity's sake, that we're doing our best to find out whether the facts on hand point toward a mass hallucination of a psychic order, like Orson Welles's "War of the Worlds" phenomena, where thousands responded with fear only because of a commanding voice on the radio, and thought they *saw* what, in fact, they only *heard*. What we're faced with here, in my opinion, is a frontal assault on our notion of reality. The only thing that makes sense is that none of the mutilations make any sense. We are faced with a challenge that could very well relate to man's survival on this planet, and every single one of our methodologies, which we pat ourselves on the back and exclaim are so unfailing and precise, has failed. We are left with a huge riddle, a Humpty-Dumpty of the twentieth century. I want to leave you with this thought: if the mutilations happened to snakes, and not cows, how many of us would be here today? And if, instead of snakes, they happened to humans, how long would the federal government have waited to spot a loophole in the laws, as Senator Salisbury so eloquently put it?"

92

Thunderous applause followed, and some members of the audience actually got up from their seats to make known their support of the final part of this speech. The senator shifted uneasily in his seat on the stage; this was more applause than his speech had gotten.

The third speaker was a Chicano cattleman who looked like a Latino Marlboro man. In a thick northern New Mexico accent, he said: "I am Arturo Ortiz from Dulce, New Mexico. I have been a cattle rancher for thirty years. I have no answers; I have only questions. My first question is why do these cattle rapes—for that is what they really are—happen only in certain places at certain times?

"I have to ask myself: was this cow that I saw alive and walking around with the rest of my herd made out of plastic? Did it have a door in its stomach that opened up so that its organs popped out and flew away into the sky? Unless I am a crazy man and need to see a doctor, those are things I saw with my own two eyes. That is all I have to say to you, except that I am hoping that someone out there knows the answers to these questions. Thank you."

He walked from the podium as a man leaves the scene of an accident. His face was wet with sweat. When he sat down, his friends placed their hands on his shoulders, and a tall boy in an identical blue and white checkered western shirt gave him a hug. There was no applause; the silence was back in the room like a deadly toxin.

The next speaker was a laboratory specialist from Los Alamos Scientific Laboratories. He was wearing a white shirt and a bola tie with a great hunk of turquoise that dwarfed his neck. He forgot to introduce himself and he moved about awkwardly behind the podium. He acted like he was on trial. He began a preamble no one in the audience could hear, and the stenographer and the honorable senator told him to raise the microphone closer to his lips. ". . . Well, the rest you know about," he said in a sudden blast that caused a shriek of feedback. "I have been investigating cases in Kansas and Nebraska, as well as New Mexico, and have gathered up a good nine years of evidence in three categories. One is predator mutilations, that would be coyotes, usually after a cattle death from another source—often just natural death like old age. The second area is a death and mutilation caused by knives or sharp instruments—very few of those in our findings. The third area is summed up by the case of these young men who were caught at the site of their crime in South Dakota. They were just a couple of kids who were cutting up cattle for the hell of it. Those are our findings. I have nothing more to add."

Professor Argyle, seated to my left, leaned over and whispered: "Some scientific method. We're going to hear a lot of cover-ups."

The next speaker, a dark, haunted figure, wasted no time when he got to the podium. "I am Tommy Barber from Brown's Station, Texas, and I have spent twenty-two years of my life studying UFO's; twelve of those years I have spent exploring the phenomena we call cattle mutilations.

"First, let me acquaint you with a few necessary facts. Some of you feel that, while something bizarre is happening, it can probably be logically explained, if not today, then presumably at some future date when we have employed a team of federal experts who really know what they're doing.

"Well, I can tell you this much, and it isn't very comforting: cattle mutilations have been going on since the early 1800s in Ireland and England. At the British Museum, there is evidence that even the great Arthur Conan Doyle attempted to solve a mysterious animal mutilation with no success. The events of recent years aren't restricted to the western United States. They're happening in Russia, Australia, New South Wales, Puerto Rico, India. Pigs, cows, sheep, rabbits, goats, and horses.

"The signs are always the same: jugular veins punctured, blood drained from the body. Just like the cases we're concerned with today. One of the most puzzling facts is that mutilated animals frequently vanish after they've been reported to the proper authorities. A mutilated calf in southeastern New Mexico was discovered by a rancher. When a team of investigators showed up only hours later, the calf had been dragged to a fence line where it just disappeared. No tracks, nothing.

"In Ohio there was a UFO sighting, and a mutilated German shepherd was found nearby. The tall grass for twenty feet around the carcass was flattened. The most dramatic event of this kind that I have on record is a steer whose head was rotated a full 360 degrees. We know of several cases where shrubs were burned in circular patterns, huge rocks moved, and even small trees pulled out by the roots. In more than one case of this kind, NORAD confirmed that 'mysterious helicopters' were picked up on radar screens and subsequently lost.

"What is really happening out there? Frankly, I don't know. But if it's not coyotes or cultists, crazy kids or the government, it must be something none of us wants to think about. I thank you."

The next speaker was a well-built black man, who gestured like a preacher from the moment he opened his mouth.

"We're all going to get browbeaten," Dr. Argyle said, "but don't let his delivery throw you. He has some interesting things to say, especially considering he is a physicist from Sandia Scientific Laboratory."

"I'm Dr. Montclaire and I'm not going to waste our time with any chitchat. I'm going to just lay it on you the way I see it. You can make of it what you will. One thing I won't do is excuse certain members of our distinguished audience because they are members of what they consider to be a persecuted minority. I am referring to the Indian population with whom I have been quarreling lately.

"I maintain that it is the responsibility of each and every one of us to get to the bottom of this thing. This is where I split paths with my Indian brothers. I say they are covering up the mutilations as fast as we're digging them up. I mean that literally. Yes, the pueblo people in the state of New Mexico are burying evidence. They say star people aren't going to like all this poking around with flashlights. I say we might as well be buried ourselves if we worry ourselves over what outer-space people think. Slide, please."

The lights dimmed, the stenographer's fingers continued to dance, and Dr. Montclaire spoke more portentously. In the dark, his voice seemed deeper and more resonant. On the screen was the head of a cow with the flesh pulled away from its face. Its teeth were the dominant image.

"This picture was taken at San Ildefonso Pueblo. We have on record the only Indian evidence that there was something very weird about this particular mutilation. An old man told us that this animal had the circle of evil influence, which means that no dog will go within fifty feet. At other mutilations a dog can be led by an Indian right up to where he could take a bite. When the circle of evil influence is present, nothing living, with the exception of humans, will go near. Not birds, not flies, only people like me who need to find out what's going on out there—what's happening on our planet? I believe there are secrets the Indians won't tell us. We should be down on our hands and knees looking on the ground instead of looking up at the stars. Thank you very much."

The lights came back on, and with them a brief shower of applause for Dr. Montclaire. He sat some distance from two Indian leaders up front who looked at him with unconcealed disdain. One of them approached the podium sternly. His voice had the sibilant native American slur that gives Indian speech its distinct rhythm.

"I speak for the Jicarilla Apache tribe. We are sick and tired of having to answer questions that have nothing to do with Indian people's problems. We're going to have to ask investigation authorities to clear themselves through our offices up at Dulce, not at the Bureau of Indian Affairs. There are certain threats that cause harm on our reservation. We want these threats to stop. We are not talking anymore until the threats stop."

He swiftly took his seat, even before Senator Salisbury came forward and asked him to disclose the nature and source of the threats.

"We are not talking until the threats stop," he said stiffly in his seat. "That is final."

13

When the *Review* was going to bed, everyone at the office stayed late. I came back from the Albuquerque mute conference to find furious activity. Marsha was busy at the computerized typesetting machine, and she didn't see me come in. Thomas, who shared my office, was at his desk going over proofs, and Jamie was at his desk correcting copy. This was no place for me to sort out thoughts, but there was no other place. If I was fast enough, I could grind out a summation of the conference.

A title came to me the moment I sat at the typewriter: "The Mute-Makers." The locals were going to get a hoot. For once it wouldn't be at their expense or mine, but at the expense of those fanatic sci-fi groupies. I could see other pieces growing out of this one called "The Alien Papers," "The Extraterrestrial Tapes," "The Cattle Caper," "The Star Surgeons."

I began to write at a stunning speed, almost flinging the typewriter off the desk at each carriage return. But the more words I put down, the less humorous the writing seemed to be. My usual clipped, sardonic style vanished. A new theme was building itself. I watched, fascinated. As a poet I had practiced automatic writing, never being sure where my next word was going to come from, but this experience was not writing at all; it was like receiving transmissions. I stopped to read my last paragraph:

A cow lying in the sun for weeks with no maggots or flies in or near the flesh is another example. These are occurrences from the Negative Plane where Evil presents itself regularly like clockwork. We need only offer our attention to this Plane and it will suck us into it. Then there are mutilations on the Positive Plane, those that cannot be explained in any other way. The clean surgical method employed by these masters of deception shows no trace of banished grace, but something spiritual has occurred when you see the muted body with missing eyes, ears, nose, or mouth. A message is being offered to us if we could only understand its meaning.

This statement had no bearing at all on my thinking. I was staring at it in a daze when the phone rang.

Static on the line, like burning bacon. Then a voice with a thick French accent said: "There is going to be a mutilation in a few minutes at San Reymo Pueblo."

"Who is this?"

"It does not matter. Have Gerald Hausman bring his camera."

"This is Gerald Hausman speaking. Who is this I am talking to?"

"No matter. You have no time to lose. There will be others there, if you don't hurry."

"What do you mean there is going to be a mutilation? Where do you get off saying such a thing? How do you know what is going to happen, or are you the perpetrator?"

"You must see what you have written," the voice said, and the contact was lost.

"Holy shit." I gathered my notebook and tape recorder, yanked the fresh sheet of typing paper with that last automatic paragraph, and headed for the door.

I passed Thomas in the hall.

"My first fresh mutilation," I told him.

"Better take along some Digel."

San Reymo Pueblo was made up of one-story adobe buildings lining a dusty road, bordered by deep green meadows. This was high country with ponderosas on the hills and higher mountains to the north towards Taos. The main cluster of adobes was on a hillside that sloped toward a deep blue lake.

I saw no Indians, and even more strangely, there were no children anywhere. Except for the dogs, the pueblo looked like it had been deserted for five hundred years. The high mountain solitude at this pueblo suggested spirits.

98

Not far from the lake's edge, ten or so people were standing beside the carcass of a brown and white bull. There was only one Indian present, the others were Spanish and Anglo. The grass had gone velvet in the light, the air hinted at frost. A mossy smell from the lake twined through the sweet pine nectar of piñon.

As I approached, one of the men, whom I recognized right away, came up and asked what I was doing there. It was Angel Gomez, and a couple feet behind him was Kreuger, his jaw set like a hawk.

"Do you remember me from a month ago?" I asked. "I'm from the *Review*. You showed me that head in the trunk of your car."

Like other Chicanos I had known, he obviously had no trouble forgetting gringo faces.

Kreuger stepped up to meet me. Gomez stood there chewing gum.

"Whose authority brought you here?" Kreuger said.

"My own, I guess."

"Don't give me that shit. This mutilation's still smoking. Who told you to come here and how'd you get here so fast?"

"Look, fella," Gomez interjected, "you got us mixed up with somebody else. This thing here is not for the press until we've evaluated it. Now you have no business here, so I suggest you run along before one of us decides you're a suspect."

"I'm not through with him yet, Angel."

Both of them were acting like true blue cops. I was sure they recognized me. That was probably why Kreuger was giving me the tough-guy routine. The whole incident seemed surreal, because I myself didn't know why I was there. Maybe I had imagined getting the summons. Maybe I was writing myself into another of those dramas that Lorry feared.

As Kreuger was preparing to give me a tongue-lashing, a tall Indian walked up to us with the bearing of a chief. These northern pueblos, San Reymo and Taos, have some real warrior types, like this man with braided hair hanging down past his chest. He was accompanied by two other people wearing blue berets. One was tall and thin and the other was short and thin. They looked very European:

99

chiseled faces with long noses and big teeth, hair unstylishly short and cut close to the ear.

The formal Indian from Picuris crossed his arms as if a portrait were about to be taken. He gave me a good looking-over, then said:

"Let this one stay. Ban the others."

"What do you mean, ban the others?" Kreuger jeered. "Let one guy in from the press before we decide how this thing happened and there'll be a swarm of these guys. Besides, this one's already written some real first-class hype. He's the last reporter you Indians ought to have around."

"He can stay," the chief said in a deep voice charged with authority.

Kreuger gave him his dirtiest scowl and headed back toward the lake where the others were gathered by the carcass. Gomez had a neutral expression. He swaggered up to me and talked out of the side of his mouth, with an eye on Kreuger.

"We gotta be careful now, kiddo," he said. "Our ass is in the sling. Len's going to be reinstated any day now, and I've been promoted to northern New Mexico's general task force field director.

"Before you put anything down on paper, better clear it with the tribe. Then you gotta wait until we get clearance from the lab; that'll be late tonight sometime. You can call me for an official press release from the state police office up in Dulce."

This guy was one hell of a ham. He was not in it for the solving of any crime; I don't think he was capable of it. He was, however, capable of responding to a situation like any good actor with a flourish of entrances and exits and a multitude of asides. He strolled off to meet the other men stooped by the lakeside, his legs bowlegged, his boots satiny in the fading light.

I turned my attention to the chief, if that's what he was, and the other two yardbirds. What a clumsy pair they were, much more comic than Kreuger and Gomez could ever aspire to be.

"Who sent you here?" the Indian asked.

"I got a call about an hour and a half ago from someone who wouldn't be identified. The person told me to get up here because something was going to happen. I only half-believed it until I got here."

"Do you believe it now?"

The short one had spoken. Bundled in a green ski parka, he was a cherub with a beret. He was the voice with the French accent on the phone.

"It was you who called. Why?"

"We want reportage without hysteria. The things you have written are good. They are not, contrary to what Mr. Kreuger says, lies. You are the only one in the papers writing what you think is spiritually true."

I thought of the satire I had been writing before the other words had come into my head and pivoted me in the opposite direction.

"Tell the truth. Tell what you see. Do not offend the Indians," the chief said.

"He won't. We promise you."

Then the chief moved in even, balanced steps toward a small queue of Indians who had gathered by the adobes at the entrance of the pueblo.

"He is a good man," the tall one said. "Afraid, but good."

"I would think, after today's hearing in Albuquerque, that the Indians would be a lot more cautious about letting us on their reservation," I said.

"You were there, too?" the tall man said. "What did you think of it?"

"I haven't had time to decide what I think. I'm trying to catch up."

The tall man laughed and offered me his hand.

"I am Harjac. Perhaps you have heard of me?"

Who hadn't heard of him? James Harjac was an international figure in the world of extraterrestrial phenomena, and I had read articles by and about him. He had led a distinguished career in physics before branching off on his own to lecture and write. He was the author of a number of scholarly books on the probability of extraterrestrial life which had received much acclaim for their mathematical accuracy. He was definitely not a UFO nut, but recently had begun expounding on his theory of Christ and the galactic federation, which cast Christ as an ancient astronaut. These latest pronouncements gathered acclaim from his devout followers, and ridicule from the scientific community. Only a month ago, Harjac had announced that he himself had been taken aboard a spacecraft, had traveled in realms beyond earthly comprehension, and had been returned to our planet to continue a mission he would soon announce to the world.

The questions I wanted to ask would have to wait; the short Frenchman was motioning us to follow him to the mutilation site. The three of us came up quietly to the small circle of six or more men who were busy batting measurements and calculations back and forth. Kreuger surveyed us with disdain, but made no move to prohibit us from watching.

"Mr. Burton, what'd you find over there?" Gomez asked.

A big man wearing buff-colored surgical gloves and a medium, gray-blue stetson was bending over the carcass of a bull. A hole had been meticulously cut in the animal's stomach, just above the genital area. All that remained of the genitalia was a dark scratch of missing fur. The hole, though, was what fascinated me. In the magenta light of early evening, the deep reddish-purple of the bull's intestinal organs showed clear to the vertebrae. The hole was like a mystic window into another world. I was overcome with an unholy attraction to this dusky scene and its grave, shadowy participants.

Then I overheard Burton say in a voice just above a whisper that the intestines had somehow been *blown out* as if by, or through, a tube.

"Some kind of blood evacuation system was pumping the animal's heart dry even as it stood there not knowing what was happening."

"You mean," Gomez said, stooping down on one knee, "that this bull was alive when it was being drained of blood?"

"Yes, and conscious, too. That is my opinion. The tests may prove otherwise."

102

"Well, how in the hell . . ."

"I don't have any answers yet. There isn't a drop of blood anywhere around here. The animal toppled over; gravity brought down its sixteen hundred pounds. The heart that was pumping blood to keep it alive emptied its system of blood. A few minutes was all it took. I don't think the bull felt a thing while it was going on. That's also an opinion, but I've been looking into the faces of bulls since I was nine years old."

"I have a bad feeling about this place," Harjac said to me.

Gomez stood up, grinning at Harjac.

"What is so bad about it?" he said chewing hard on his gum.

"For one thing, this lake is surrounded with owls and spirits. It's no accident there's been a mutilation here, and the Indians know it."

"I bet I know more about owls than you'll ever know," Gomez said in a haughty Spanish way. "My grandmother told my brother and me that when you saw an owl with a red face, you'd better get home, because that was the devil." He let out a howl of laughter. "Well, the Apaches up in Dulce say a man can travel in the form of an owl, but that's medicine-man talk. When it comes to mumbo jumbo owl talk, I don't listen anymore. I was raised Catholic; I believe in God, the Holy Ghost, and all the rest of it."

"As do I," Harjac said, "but I also believe that Christ, the Lord, came here from a world that was light-years away. He came to save us, but we wouldn't let him. Now, before our eyes, is proof of another power. We should not assume that it is intrinsically evil. It symbolizes power, that is all."

"Well, you got me, professor," Gomez said, rolling his eyes to indicate to Burton and the others that Harjac was cracked. "I can't disagree with what you say. Fact is, I don't understand what the hell you said. I'm just a dumb cop and you are a doctor of something or other. Well, put it all into your report. That's what you're here for."

Gomez, Burton, and Kreuger moved off from the rest of us and conversed in inaudible tones. I faced Harjac by moving into the place vacated by Gomez. I looked directly into his eyes and saw that he was crazy—overbred, overread, and underfed. No matter: Harjac was himself as interesting a mute as the bull without a stomach.

"I found what you said extremely interesting. I'd like to hear more about what you think happened here."

"They don't understand what I tell them. They pay me to make foolish reports."

"Who's they?"

"I work for NASA. I am also the executive director of the Academy for Cosmic Research in California. My mutilation studies are probably too ethereal for these flatfoots to comprehend. I really don't care what they think, as long as they continue to let me reach the media."

"I don't quite follow."

It was impossible to believe that he was a charlatan. He obviously believed everything he said. He removed his beret for a moment, revealing a small scar that meandered into his hairline.

"Ironic," he laughed. "I work for NASA, yet I have been commissioned by the Galactic Federation to carry on my work here on earth. Do you see this scar? It was put there by beneficent beings who put me through a series of tests. The scar was done by a man's fingers. It is my awakening mark. One day we will all have them."

"You were saying before about your 'work on earth'—what is meant by that?"

"Why, my purpose, of course, was *awakened* to help awaken others. NASA helps me to do this by paying for my research even though I think they think I'm crazy. For the time being, and that may only be for a short while, they let me carry on my work because it looks good. The hypocrites like to appear open-minded. Without me they would all look like desperate little bigots."

"How do mutilations tie in with your work? I don't see the connection."

"To you and the others here, these mutilations must seem horrid. That is because you do not understand what is behind them. You fear they are the work of dangerous aliens, when in reality, they are only intimations of the power of peace."

104

"If they're messages—isn't that what you're suggesting?—then why aren't we understanding them?"

"We will in time. There are many types of mutilations. Some are the work of visitors from the Negative Plane, the plane of the Antichrist, and those are frightening. A cow lies dead in the hot sun for weeks with no maggots or flies. Such mutilations are to be shunned, for there is nothing we can learn from them, but the others, like this one here today, are a spiritual message. A message from where? We think everything bizarre comes from the sky, but these mutilations on Indian land, always near stretches of water, have proven to me that our visitors are often from within."

I was amazed that the phrases he was using were the same ones I had written in my office, but there wasn't time for reflection. "From within you say? What do you mean by that?"

"They originate within the earth and appear above the earth at a later time. The Picuris have known about inner space for hundreds of years. They have withheld this information because we are not adequately prepared to understand. What would you say if I told you we could travel in inner space by finding an unknown passage in this very lake?"

"Getting back to what you said before, I still don't see what a mutilated animal has to do with spirituality. I've studied all kinds of religions and have never come across that idea."

"You're mistaken, but that is natural. At first it's hard to accept. I could show you Tibetan Buddhist tankas that clearly indicate flesh being flayed by gods for a greater purpose. All passages to worlds of the spirit involve the shedding of flesh and its earthly ties. The ancient Hindus said that nothing exists or is destroyed; things merely change shape or form. So what is so surprising about a mutilated horse or cow? Humans have done it in religious ceremonies for thousands of years. It is just as Christ was prepared for his cycle of eternal return."

"Mutilated cattle are not my idea of anything divine."

"We pass through many incarnations. The first Tibetans were

monkeys with tails and their ancestors are the yetis—or what we on this continent call Bigfoot.

"In Asia, long ago, there was a hidden kingdom, a place of broad lakes that have since turned to sand. Here in northern New Mexico there is also sand, but the lakes remain, and so do their caretakers the Indians, who facially, culturally, esoterically, and in every other way harken back to the ancient monkey kings of Tibet."

In the moonlight shone the lake and the white bull lying on its side.

"You will have to leave now," Kreuger said. "This investigation is over."

I walked to the car with Harjac and the other little man. They said nothing. As we neared the place where cars were parked, the small Frenchman thrust his hand toward me.

"My name is Etienne," he said. "If you are studying these things, we will see more of each other."

Harjac walked into the night without saying good-bye.

"I wouldn't want to be him," I said. "He must carry quite a burden."

"Yes, he does."

"Are you part of his research group?"

"No. He took me along as a favor. Now I see that he only knows this much, and it is all a little to one side, if you understand my meaning."

In the dark, this small Frenchman seemed more a person from another world than old man Harjac, who had all the answers in the palm of his hand.

"What do you do for a living?"

"I have a Center for Psychic Phenomena in Santa Fe, where my friends come and speak. One of the speakers, a very close friend who grew up on the Hopi Reservation, has a view similar to Harjac's. She knew him and introduced us. You must come and hear her talk on the Hopi prophecy."

"I never heard of it. What is it?"

"The Hopis say they came from the stars, originally."

106

"Just like the Navajos who say they came from under ground but were helped by star people."

"Harjac believes in both myths."

"And you?"

"I think humans have only one hope for the future—to get off this burning cinder of a planet as soon as possible."

Part Three
Nightworkers

14

Now I was into the second month of the probe, and my second major piece about to appear in the *Review:* "Hunting with Harjac: On the Trail of the Mutes." The galleys were on my desk, the essay having been hammered out furiously the night before at the office after I got back from San Reymo. Marsha had typeset it somewhere between two and three in the morning.

I could predict the response. It had the good clean taste of cold sake in a clay cup. I presented Harjac no holds barred, and I went out of my way to show how hypocritical NASA was to keep such a man on their payroll. At the same time, I backhandedly complimented them for their effort, because it was my contention that a man like Harjac, crazy though he may appear, often can see the truth while "normal" ones cannot. Maybe I was a little hard on the old boy. Maybe I was so angry over having to write about mutes that I needed someone to punish. That freak phase of automatic writing that I had been put through by who knows who—maybe Harjac himself—was in itself enough to get me into an H. L. Mencken mood. Well, at least I wasn't going to have to listen to hicks putting me down for supporting weird theories. In a few hours the *Review* would be out, and I would get a laurel wreath for satiric newswriting instead of a barrage of crank calls.

I settled in with the latest articles from the clipping bureau we subscribed to and sipped a mug of coffee while waiting for the rest of the office to show up for work.

There were some funny clippings, as well as the usual, and there were a few additional tie-ins to recent mutes. A young Indian claimed to have seen a "bright light in the East that looked like a blazing star that moved" the night before a mutilation at Santa Clara.

Another Pueblo family from Taos—mother, daughter, father, uncle, and 112-year-old grandmother—had confessed to the county sheriff's department that for several days prior to a mutilation down by the river they had witnessed blue lights. When asked why they had not discussed the lights with anyone, the family lapsed into characteristic silence. They would not comment on whether they thought the lights were earthly or extraterrestrial. It was thought, as a tribal policeman named Naranjo had stated, that the family had been "afraid to speak of the lights and were superstitious about them coming back."

The *Rio Grande Sun* had an interview with Angel Gomez, in which he said the latest lab reports confirmed his suspicion that mutilated animals were being bled to death by inserting twelve- to fourteen-gauge needles into their jugular veins. The beating of the animals' hearts forced blood into a container hooked up to the needles. Prior to the bleeding, Gomez said, the animals were anesthetized by a depressant. He quoted from a recent lab report: "In the anesthetized or wholly sedated animal, the heart will continue to function and act as a pump until the last drops of blood have been drained. The method of death is nothing out of the realm of human capacity."

The reason many cases had been getting overnight lab analyses,

Gomez said, was because the carcasses they were finding were only hours old when discovered. They offered an ideal opportunity to inspect for chemical residue.

Recent testing had also proved that an anticoagulant which Gomez said "any chemist could fix" was used to rush the blood through the jugular veins. Bones around shoulders appeared to have been shattered, suggesting the animals had been dropped from the air.

I wondered how the lab report on the San Reymo mute had turned out. I decided to call Gomez myself, as he had offered to let me hear the lab report when it came in from Sandia. I dialed the State Police Headquarters on the Jicarilla Apache Reservation up in Dulce, New Mexico, where Gomez had his obscure office.

An Indian answered in a low, flat, stones-rubbing-together voice and said that Gomez would be right with me. I waited for what seemed an hour but was probably only a few minutes while the Apache adjusted his feathers, and then I heard Gomez growling like Zorba the Greek. This amazing man was an assemblage of characters all rolled into one. He could sound as tough, as innocent, as smart, or as ignorant as the next fellow, and somehow always managed to seem authentic. I was going to have to do some required reading on the background of Angel Gomez.

"Whaddya want?" he snapped into the phone.

I explained who I was and that I was interested in the lab report from the bull at San Reymo.

"Not all in yet," he snapped again.

"Can you tell me what *is* in? You offered that last night."

"Who the hell are you again?" he said.

He sounded drunk, but I'd seen him act like this perfectly sober so I knew better.

"Hausman, the guy you stopped coming out of Los Alamos, remember? I was there last night."

"Oh, yeah, why didn't you say so? You were talking with that Frenchy. Well, okay, I'll give you what I've got but it ain't much, not yet anyway. They tell me down at Sandia that the tongue on this one showed signs of burning, like it had been fried in hot fat. They also found clamp marks on the hind legs, which kind of confirms what I've been saying all along about these animals getting lifted off their feet while they're still standing."

"You mean you think the mutilation was done in the air?"

"That's a damn good possibility. What we know for sure is that the mutilation takes place after what they call anesthetization and exsanguination—putting 'em to sleep and draining their blood. There was no blood anywhere around the place where the animal fell, so again we think it's gotta be happening up there in the sky."

"Any blood spots found anywhere at all?"

"Just a few on the carcass itself."

"What color were they, brown or black or what?"

"Normal blood from a mutilation should be a dark purple color, or like you say maybe even black, but this stuff on the hide, and there was very little of it, was bright, almost neon, pink."

"Can you put your finger yet on what that suggests about the mutilation process?"

"Hey, you ask a lot of questions."

"That's my job."

"Well, my job is to catch the perpetrators of this crime, and I don't want to spend the rest of the week talking to a newsman about hypothetical blood colors."

Now I was talking to a new incarnation of Inspector Gomez. Kreuger or someone like him had probably just walked into his office.

"Well, thanks for the information."

"Here's something you can print if you want to," Gomez offered. "Tell them Gomez says whoever's out there has some pretty sophisticated scissors. They ought to like the way that sounds."

He clicked off. There was going to have to be a Gomez interview soon, but I wanted to hold off until he had laid all the cards on the table. Following this mute case was like reading a detective novel; the longer I stayed with it, the more I knew, but the less I seemed to know about how it was happening. At the moment, I was considering whether the mutilations could be the work of a deadly, bored—no pun intended—policeman. There was a nice angle: "Gomez Bores through Gore for More."

I returned to my clippings from the other New Mexico newspapers. There was a variety of stories on subjects that might be related to mutilation. The *New Mexican* headlined "Solar Balloons Cause Sante Fe UFO Scare." Two giant pieces of black and white inflatable plastic with a snowflake design had been seen close to San Ildefonso Pueblo, "lumbering at low altitudes toward the Rio Grande." Cars lined the highways from Camel Rock to Nambe to witness the long bubbles that reflected the noonday sun. The mystery was traced to an Australian-born batik artist, Geoff Jarvis, who was working with the Northern Pueblo Agency's Arts Experience Program. The thirty-foot-long "big plastics," being shown off to Pueblo children as solar balloons, were not expected to take so readily to the air.

The *Torrance County Citizen* reported that a weird light had been seen blinking on a hill at one-minute intervals. This was later discovered to be the light at the end of a pivoting irrigation system.

There was a missing son story in the *Roswell Daily Record*. An Air Force second lieutenant was in a telephone booth when the line went dead. According to observers, the young man vanished. "Harley was very strong in his religious convictions," his father commented to the press. "He had just bought a house in Albuquerque and was going to hold Bible studies there. We can only pray that he is not being harmed."

A letter in the *Albuquerque Journal* also caught my fancy:

CATTLE MUTILATION NOT MYSTERY

My father owned land east of Roy, three miles north of Solano, where I was born. I remember that in 1910, east of Roy, there was nothing but prairies, and often one could see a sheepherder's tent up on the hills, as it was mostly sheep grazing land. At that time, I recall a cattle rancher, Vidal Martinez, who owned several hundred head of cattle and they would pasture east of Roy.

In those days I saw many cows mutilated near water lakes. The reason was that in those lakes there was plenty of vegetation inside the water which would bring all kinds of bugs and water spiders; cows have the habit of getting in the lake to drink water and would swallow these spiders, so they would swell up and if there was no one around to help them, they would die. First the vultures would pick out their eyes and tongue, then coyotes and other animals would get their genitals and rectum, where the hide is soft and thin. When biting off the flesh they use their molars, making a clean cut, and since the cow is already dead, there is no blood pressure. I also know this cow mutilation happens only at certain times in the summer . . .

"Boo," said Marsha behind me, and I jumped a foot out of my chair.

"I'm sorry, Ger," she said in that husky monotone voice, "but you have to deal with that person in the lobby."

"What person?"

"That guy who's always trying to sell you the story of Jesus on Horseback is back again."

"Show him in."

Marsha's surprised eyes were telling me what I should have recalled: that the old Bataan March Veteran in the lobby, who seemed to make a living by haunting newspaper offices with his dusty tales, actually smelled worse than his stories.

"Let me dump him out the door for you and you can see him outdoors later."

"No, show him in. For once I can use him."

"He's back there," she said down the hallway and in another moment, the *viejo* came into my office, dragging one foot and apologizing for his intrusion. He crushed a sweat-begrimed stetson in one hand and held a hand-carved cane in the other. His oval face was moon-pocked and striated with microscopic veins. His eyes were not only cataracted, but socketed in different directions so he looked at you as if you were in two places at once.

"There's something you can do for me, and I will pay you for it. The story about Jesus on Horseback, I want to hear all of it."

116

"On my grandmother's soul, that story is true," he wheezed, his eyes roving ceiling and floor.

"Can you describe the man in white for me?"

"Oh, no. I did not see him. My grandmother saw him with her own eyes when he rode into Santa Fe on his big, big white horse—ten hands high."

"How big was the man?"

"Big, like the horse. My grandmother told me that all around this man was a ring of light, such as you see in Santa Fe after a big rain and the sun comes from behind the clouds."

"What did the man do when he came to town?"

"He cared for people. He was a great healer. This man was no ordinary human being."

"Do you believe he was Jesus Christ?"

"I could not say that for sure."

"Well, did your grandmother say he was Jesus Christ?"

"She did say that," he coughed into a closed fist. His fogged eyes continued to rove the room. "My grandmother, she told me when I was very sick one time that he would come and cure me. She said he would only come to our house if I prayed to Jesus. So I always think to myself that this man was Jesus, only I think he did not have the same face that our Lord had when he walked on earth. My grandmother said this man was very tall and he had white hair and a yellow beard."

"Did he appear when you prayed?"

"No, but I had a dream about him. He rode out of the sky on a blazing star. He blessed all the earth and all earthly creatures, and he said that he lived up in Heaven and could not come back to us anymore. Then I woke up and my fever had broken."

"Was that the only time you dreamed about him?"

"No, there was one other time when I was older. I used to ride up into the mountains to check my grandfather's cattle. I would pass a big old house inhabited by three women who were witches. When I rode by, one of these women would always come out and ask me to come inside for coffee. Being a little scared, I ignored her and kept on riding. One day when I passed the house, that woman came out and beckoned. As usual, I passed on by her, but when I was out of sight, I heard her calling my name.

"I turned around and saw a coyote following me. There was no one in sight but the coyote, so I just kept on riding. The sound of that woman calling stayed in my mind. Again I turned and saw that it was the coyote, so I took my gun out and I wounded the coyote, left it there dying.

"The next day I was doing some errands in town, and I heard that one of the witches had been shot and wounded the day before. When I told my grandmother this story, she gave me a little brown bag with a *cachana* root inside it that would ward off *brujos* and *brujas*. I had been touched by the Devil's witchery. Then I dreamed the man on horseback came and blessed me, and I was alright again.

"My grandmother also gave me an *osha root* to put into my boot whenever I was clearing brush."

"What was that for?"

"*Osha* keeps away rattlesnakes, and it is good against witches."

"Is there another name for the *cachana* root?"

The old man rasped with a watery smile, "They call it blazing star."

15

For lunch that day I celebrated with *chiles rellenos*, chiles peeled and fried in a batter with egg and flour, stuffed with cheese, and served with beans and rice; *sopapillas*, blowups of fried dough into which you pour butter and honey; and three or four cups of scalding coffee. I had not allowed myself to indulge in a special lunch for a long time, but for the time being, Atkins was off my case, a noncontroversial story was being printed, and I had a score of leads for interesting articles that would in no way put my neck in a noose. I felt good for once.

After lunch I strolled around the plaza, watched the Indians sell their wares in front of the Palace of the Governors, followed the pigeons from eave to eave, and breathed in the autumn air. The first snow had already hit the high mountains. Elk season was on, the great shaggy bodies pinned to the roofs of stationwagons and stuffed into the back of pickups. This was the season I liked best. Meandering in the sun that warms the soul as well as the skies in New Mexico, I knew I had been too preoccupied these last couple of months.

I hung around the office all that day without doing much of anything except keeping out of Jamie Atkins's sight and ruminating about the old man's words. What he had said tied in with some of the things that Harjac and Etienne had said. There seemed to be a connection between the sacred, or what was thought to be sacred in the old southwest, and the profane. I was toying with the notion that the mutilations might be seen as a blood-wedding of the two.

I decided not to lay off the extraterrestrial theory until I had gone over it again. Perhaps another visit to the southwest archives at the state library would be a start. I headed across town. The gnome of a librarian disappeared into the gloomy stacks for a Bureau of Ethnology Report for the year 1933. Without looking too far, I unearthed the Cherokee legend of the star people.

The hunters were camping in the mountains one night when they saw two lights moving along a distant ridge. They watched and wondered. They saw them the next night and the next. On the third morning they crossed to the ridge and found two creatures round and large with fine gray fur and little heads like those of terrapins. When the breeze played upon the fur, showers of sparks flew out.

The hunters kept them several days. At night they would grow bright and shine; by day they were balls of gray fur, except when the wind stirred and the sparks flew out. They were quiet and no one thought of their trying to escape, but on the seventh night they rose from the ground like balls of fire above the tree tops climbing higher and higher until they were only bright points. The hunters then knew they were stars.

My mind went back to Etienne's remark about the Hopi prophecy, and I thought about the Navajo emergence myth as well.

What are myths anyway, but the deep dreams of an ancient people. We modern people have our own myths, too, our supermen and Frankensteins and Count Draculas. That got me thinking again about mutilation blood, and how blood can be a symbol of good or evil.

There was an Indian devil-saint who appeared in a blaze of light, like a star, seized whomever he chose, and gashed them with sharp flint. He drew out their entrails and healed them at the same time. He could break and set limbs as quick as he could look at them, because the moment he put a hand on a wound that he had made, it was blessed. He appeared often as a man, but also as a woman, and he was known to climb into a house and make it go up into the sky.

If ever there was a place where impossible things happened not once but twice, it was New Mexico. Much later, the Spanish had come, driven by a clawing need for gold. They beat it out of the pueblos only to find that gold to the Indians was merely stores of corn or feathers. Those insane explorers were struck with vision that could not be shaken loose by truth. Yet there was one who was different: Cabeza de Vaca, a conquistador turned saint who, naked and barefoot, healed thousands of Indians with a brush of his hand.

"The wound I make," said Cabeza de Vaca, "appears only like a seam in the palm of the hand." Yet moments before, it had been a gash into the chest of a dying Indian. He said the power passed through him from God. So while his brothers cut off Indian hands as payment for misbehavior, Cabeza de Vaca made other injured

Indians whole and claimed no credit. I felt that I was onto something interesting. A new article was brewing.

That evening after leaving the library, I phone Etienne and arranged to meet him at his new Center for Psychic Research. I knocked on the door (otherwise unmarked) that bore the number he had given me. He himself answered the door, a wan man with a waiflike smile and angled eyes and ears. His skin looked transparent in the sudden burst of light that filled the dark corridor.

"Come in," he said. "I have been expecting you."

The only furniture in the spacious, well-lit room was a case full of books about UFO's, religion, and shamanistic studies. There was an oriental carpet, a small devotional stand with a candle and incense holder, and a few plump pillows. Etienne sat down on one of these and, after pointing out that I had forgotten to remove my shoes at the door (there was a small sign on the wall making the request), began to describe an unusual operation that he had been given only a few weeks before.

"You asked on the telephone about my knowledge of psychic healing," he began in his thick French accent. "Well, I don't know very much more than what I have observed. Recently, my tonsils were so inflamed that I could not eat or sleep. I could not speak because of the pain.

"First I tried acupuncture, but that did me no good. The pain got worse and worse, until I had no strength left at all. Then I hear of a Philippino healer, who has brought about many cures all over the world. I call him and he says—just like this—'Yes, you come right away.'

"My wife drives me to Albuquerque, where he will treat me at someone's home, because the American Medical Association will not let him practice. When I first look on this man, I know he has incredible powers, but there is nothing unusual about his movements except that he seems to be in a light trance. He tells me, 'I don't guarantee anything. I am nothing by myself. I am not the Healer. I carry the Light of Christ and His Father. What is your trouble?'

"He looks in my throat like he is seeing into me with X-ray

vision. When I mention this to him he tells me, for a joke, what color underwear I am wearing. I laugh even though it is painful for me, because he has guessed correctly.

"He says to me, 'Lie on the table and pray to God!' Then he cuts my throat from ear to ear with his thumb. I feel warm blood on my neck. I see it on his hands as he wipes them with a clean cloth. Then he places one hand on my forehead and the other on the center of my chest. This, he explains, is to make the energy flow again between my forehead and abdomen. I feel a natural current vibrating in my body. He tells me that the rest is up to me. I must now try to help myself. I have no voice at all. The whole operation lasted two and one-half minutes. In a day's time, I am completely healed.

"When I went to see him again, for a different complaint, he finished the operation by breathing very gently all over my body. I felt that I was full of strong, positive energy. After that, I gave up smoking and drinking. I could never touch either of them again. I remember when I thanked him, I suddenly burst into tears and could not stop. They just kept flowing and flowing, cleansing my body and soul. It was then that he told me that he had been to many strange places during his life. He spoke personally to me, man to man."

"What kind of places did he speak of?"

"He told me that he had just returned from Atlantis and that that was where he had first learned how to heal people with his hands."

16

My article "Mystery Healing: A Holy or Unholy Art" got a positive response from a segment of the community I hardly knew existed until I met Etienne and saw his center. During the first flurry of morning calls, Jamie Atkins asked whether I myself had ever mutilated anything.

"You mean, am I the mysterious mutilator of Tesuque?"

"No, I am asking you whether you ever mutilated a living thing in your life."

"Of course not, don't be ridiculous."

He was goading me, but might just be pulling my leg. I decided to throw his question back at him.

"How about you, pal, you ever mutilated anything?"

"Let's see," he said, sitting on the corner of his desk. He felt the knot in his tie to make sure it corresponded perfectly with his collar: dead center. "Yes, I can think of several mutilations for which I myself have been responsible. This morning I was guilty of mutilating a pig. Last night, sorry to say, I had a hand in mutilating a lamb."

"There's nothing mystic about chewing, salivating, and swallowing."

"No?"

"No. Look, Jamie, will you please not waste my morning with grounders out in left field? For once I have a notion of what I ought to be doing."

"I have news for you. You've started something out there with this series of guess who or guess what articles. I like it, always have, and I don't care how much criticism we get as long as you follow through, but you have no business raising questions and not answering them to the best of your ability. Otherwise we are just teasing the public."

Oh, pain, pain, I thought. What diabolical scheme do I have to delve into now? He's going to ask me to mutilate a cow.

"What I'm getting at, Gerry, is that most of us are mutilators ourselves. We may not all wield the knife, but each and every one of us is guilty of eating living matter, or matter that was once alive. What's the difference between a vegetarian and a meat eater? Degree, that is all. Vegetarians say that green things don't yell as loud when they're pulled out of the ground as cattle do when they're punched with a butcher blade."

"We are evil, no denying it. Now how is any of this going to get another article written?"

"In this recent piece, if I read you right, you are suggesting that the means with which healings take place are similar to the methods of certain mutilations. Is that correct?"

"I said it."

"So I'm asking you, as always, to follow through. If it's a matter of belief, go into the belief. Who believes it? What, and why, and when did they believe it? You have hinted at something I have been thinking about for a long time: Penitentes, skinwalkers. You worked on the Navajo Reservation for a period of time, didn't you? Well, explore all those dimensions. What do the Indians think of mutilations? How about the sun ceremonies of the Mandan or the flesh-piercing rituals of the Crow? Didn't one of those tribes raise a body up into the air by stabbing a wooden wedge into the pectoral muscles and tying a pulley to that wedge? I've seen pictures of bodies, George Catlin, I believe painted some, hanging ten or twelve feet off the ground. Isn't that what you would call a mutilation?"

"For a kind of divine purpose, however."

"What is the purpose of a child's torturing a worm with a stick until its guts come out? Haven't we all done something like that at one time or another? How about putting a firecracker into a frog's mouth; I knew plenty of kids back in Mississippi who did that. One guy I knew planted little chicks up to their necks in the ground and ran over them with a lawn mower. What for?"

"Because he could do it and get away with it."

"Don't get me wrong, Gerry. I appreciate your efforts very much. I think that last healing story is the best thing you've done, but you've got to clinch your point. When lightning bolts like that are flying around in the air, they're dangerous. Once grounded, they're harmless."

"Alright, you want historical, anthropological, mystical, and psychological facts on the mutilations. You want to see some human

124

blood in there, too, don't you? Okay, now I think I know what you want. You want me to go under the skin, so to speak."

"You don't have to do interviews for that stuff. Piles of primary material are over at the State library. Wolves that walked the streets of Santa Fe with hoods over their heads, accurately described by people who saw them. I want you to go from healing hands to the boundaries of Hell. Go to the edge and look over. What's the worst—report on it. Then go back to the flatfooted plane we're supposed to be living on, and tell what's happening here. That's an assignment further down the line."

Atkins was a contradictory son of a bitch. He feinted and tucked until he got just what he wanted. I promised myself to lay him out one of these days, but that too was a future assignment.

What angered me was that I thought I had already done what he was asking me to do. I looked over my healing articles and saw that in one respect he was right; there was little or no gore. That was how they seemed to me.

Probably one reason why I had avoided blood and guts was that deep down I believed in the nobility of man. I resisted the facts when they said that people out in the dead of night were exhibiting deviant behavior. I would rather turn away from criminality and call it something else. Perverse healing was okay with me because it could be flipped over to see its opposite aspect of holiness.

Now Jamie wanted blood dripping on ceilings and people screaming. It might jam my joints to gear up for bloodletting, but if that's what he wanted, he would get it—if I could find it.

Jamie had asked about the Penitentes. I knew what they were about, and I did not think it was evil. I remembered that night up in the Gallinas Canyon with Lorry. We were near a morada that Holy Thursday, and the singing was in the air. It was not an intonation of evil, but something as holy as the rock that hemmed us in and shut out the stars.

When the first Spanish settlers came into the mountain highlands to farm and live in peace, they brought with them everything that they had known in colonial Spain. Their religion governed lives as it always had, but here in New Mexico, the sacred was twisted a new way. In the high canyons the moradas of the brothers of light were born. These men had not less, but more faith than their predecessors in Spain, and wedded to their belief were the phantasmagoric shapes around them: the claw marks of a big cat on the wine-colored bark of a juniper, the fastidiousness of the cholla's house of thorns and wax-bright candlelit blossoms, the inescapable treachery of the moaning wind, the animal rapture of the Pueblo dances. The Indians they had conquered practiced a faith older than time and as consoling and unbreakable as canyon stone burnished with lichen. Spanish and Indian faiths seem to have rubbed off on one another.

On the night that I first heard them, I thought the wind itself was speaking to me. That must have been how it had all started. The wind had spoken to the Penitentes, and they had given the wind their bodies and souls. In the early days, they had reenacted the crucifixion, complete with death and bleeding. The landscape warranted such devotion, and the old religion fell away as it met the mad eye of the new. The Penitentes were brothers of suffering. They asked no praise or reward for their love of God and their triumph over the body, but what they got when the Church, in all its rigid majesty, heard about their flailings of whips and cactus clubs, was excommunication. So the warped seedling mellowed into an artful rendering of truth, and became a misfit. People were afraid of it.

At the state library I dug again for the words of witches, Penitentes, and other prisoners of flesh that offered glimpses into a world of half-light where madness repeatedly verged on revelation. Again and again, I found that cause and cure, reason and unreason, were two sides of the same coin.

I remembered reading about the witches that appeared as fireballs, for instance. Neither meteor nor comet, these bright orange disks sometimes turned gray, blue, or pale white and passed silently through the sky. Sometimes they appeared thunderous and took giant strides upon the earth, or clustered like small birds in the dead limbs of a winter-branched cottonwood.

Once two girls spent the night with an old woman who lived in their village. Late at night they heard a peculiar noise and got up to investigate. The old woman had left her bed and was seen applying a strange ointment to her naked body, face and arms. Muttering some incomprehensible words, the old woman exploded into an orange fireball and shot up the chimney.

A newspaper clipping told of a family in Taos whose home had been bombarded by fireballs in full view of neighbors and police.

Stones accompanying the lights came out of the night sky and hailed the roof. In keeping with the traditional belief in sorcery, the neighbors formed a circle around the home with lanterns to protect it (this is said to attract a witch and confine her in a limited space where she can be captured and made human) but throughout the night the stones and fireballs rained down in pure evil. In the morning the stones stopped.

When witches danced their circle dance, the movement was of fireballs in a forest or meadow. To trap them, what was needed was a circle of lanterns, an ordered series of flames that would end the chaos of leaping light.

Through the centuries in the hidden canyons and caves of the Rio Grande, in dimly lit adobes or mountain moradas, nightworkers carried on their holy or unholy missions. The devil himself chose a place where four roads met on the shores of a lake for his sabbat. The cloven feet of demons made this spot barren. Yet it was the circle, the shape of a lake, that could entrap a witch and allow the disembowelment of her power. A circular body of water, renowned for its purity, could also let an ensorcered person seek the identity of the sorcerer, whose image would float to the surface like an innocent fish:

In the center of the small place was a limpid pool. Juan sat her down and bade her to look into the pool until a face appeared. She would recognize the face, he said, and at that instant, her mind would be wholly restored.

Then Juan dropped his knife into the water and sat down beside her. In time the troubled water calmed and together they gazed steadfastly into its clear depths until they could see the face of the one who had bewitched her.

Whatever was wrong could be made right again by the proper application of that wrong. Good blood and bad blood were always used for holy and unholy ceremonies. When the Penitentes shed blood they tried to transcend dishonor and sin and to achieve beatitude through suffering:

> Flynn moved close enough to see the entire covering of flesh had been torn from the body of the whippers, leaving the ribs exposed. The Penitente's back looked as though sharp knives had been drawn across it in all directions and the flesh torn out with pincers. When the bad blood was gone, the good blood could begin to flow.

Good blood was used to lure a Santo Domingo witch, who came in the form of a coyote:

> He was all naked. He told them to put blood all over his body. They got blood and put it all over his body. It was human blood and pretty soon old coyote came down the path howling terribly. But when he smelled the blood he kept quiet and they were able to catch him.

In 1896, a terrible epidemic ravaged the pueblos of the Rio Grande. At Cochiti, the sickness was attributed to witchcraft. Spies were appointed to watch the church and cemetery day and night. Two dogs, one white and one black, were seen wandering the outskirts of the pueblo. Then one night shortly after midnight, a man appeared. His body was painted white with black hands, and black rags were tied to his shoulders. Once caught he was discovered to be a *koshare*, a pueblo clown, who died, as soon as he was pinned to the ground, in "floods of blood." The epidemic ceased.

Good and evil rode the same horse in these stories of New

Mexico past, and only belief separates the two. When bad times befell the pueblo of Cochiti, the watchers of evil kept their eyes on the church as well as the cemetery. The white and black motif was unified in the costume of the clown, but he himself had broken his traditional role to perform evil.

In many Indian legends, good is not confused with evil, but the two are often embodied in the same person or thing, as in that familiar of all worlds, Coyote the cosmic bungler. Coyote represents both witchcraft and wisdom, transformer and trickster. A clue to the cattle with missing parts: Coyote lost his eyes only to gain them. He proved that things that come from the stars were earthly in origin. The Pueblos, and all other American Indians, respected Coyote as a devil of a friend, knowing that he was only themselves in a trick of fur, or that they were just like him in a trick of skin.

17

The night I was hit by the motorcycle, something else happened that I have never forgotten: the appearance during my recuperative period of Joe Rae, a Navajo who had become my good buddy when we were in college together. At the moment I had been struck down in the road, J. R. knew about it. I have never forgotten the patient way that he stayed by my bed. His nut-brown countenance resembled a Tibetan priest's. The eyes almost always smiled before the lips, wrinkles filling the corners of those haunted, slanted eyes.

I have often thought that J. R.'s presence may have helped to knit my wrecked bones. If so, he was merely returning a favor. A year before the accident, J. R. attended a party with me, got drunk on a glass of red wine, and pinned a girl named Rhonda to the floor. It took four of us to disentangle J. R. from Rhonda, and two of us—my roommate Pat and me—to carry J. R. home. We were stopped once by the local police, who always had it in for drunk Indians, but in the dark with J. R. propped between us, we looked like three good old boys laughing each other home arm in arm.

Once in our room, we loosened J. R.'s clothes, put him to bed in a spare bunk, and saw to it he was breathing easily before turning out the lights. I had never in my life seen anyone so dead drunk except maybe a dead man. In the night, an Apache who had followed us out of sight to our doorstep, jimmied the door open and tiptoed into the bedroom. I sat up in my bed and saw this crazy Apache beating J. R. with a wet towel while trying to queer him. Pat and I wrestled the bastard to the floor and kicked him out into the night with a threat we'd kill him if he returned. He fled with one of our sheets draped over his head to hide his identity, but we were able to report him the next day to the dean who expelled him for good.

J. R. awoke the next morning knowing nothing of the attempted Apache pillage of his person. He even seemed to feel chipper. He said he was fit enough to accompany us to the Museum of the Palace of the Governors on the Plaza in Santa Fe where there was an Anasazi pottery exhibit. All went smoothly until J. R. got into the Anasazi room. Suddenly, and without any warning, he tossed his cookies into a six hundred-year-old, three-foot-high Pueblo water jar. The sound of his retching brought a guard and a janitor in full pursuit, eyes peeled for a withered old wino. They saw only three college boys, well-attired and beaming, pens making tracks in open notebooks.

In the stately hall, however, vented the smell of rotten wine mixed with sour food.

"I didn't mean to puke on my ancestors," J. R. said when we were back out in the sunshine. Then he thanked us for getting him home to our place alive the night before. He knew he'd been crocked out of his skull.

130

Unlike any Navajo I had ever met, J. R. was a throwback, a medicine man without any magic. Later on, I found out why. His family had fought hard against the corrosion of white society, and had kept to the old ways.

J. R.'s father was a holy man, a *stargazer*. In the old days he would look into the sky and see the future and the way the tribe should go; quietly and suddenly, the tribe would break camp and be gone. The stargazer said who would live and who would have to die. J. R.'s grandfather had been a scout who went after Geronimo. Long years later at over a hundred years of age, this hero had been buried at Arlington.

It was through J. R. that I had first learned of the skinwalkers, the werewolves of the Navajo. J. R.'s old man had seen them looking in at the smoke hole of his hogan. He had also fallen under one's spell by wearing a wolfskin he had found in a hollow tree. J. R. said these wolves that walked on two legs could move faster than a car. They were magic.

I never would have heard anything about them, or about any seasonal Navajo songs or dances, had it not been for our friendship born of an Apache-ousting and the ceremony of the Anasazi jar. J. R. never touched another drop of alcohol after that night, and he prayed for me during my operation, after I went down under those screaming tires.

Fifteen years had gone by without another contact. Then a few weeks ago, he had just showed up in Santa Fe for a talk. He had not changed a bit, except that he had a wife named Ethel and two children. His manner was as quiet, easy, and as knowing as ever.

"Sometime, you'll meet my father," he told me. "Sometime soon."

That turned out to be sooner than I thought, and to a greater purpose than I could have dreamed. The whole family showed up unannounced at my house just after Jamie gave me the blood ultimatum. J. R.'s father sat far back in his chair, gray stetson on his knees, and stared at the ceiling. His mother crouched at the edge of her seat as if she were ready to run for cover. The old man spoke no

English, but she spoke it exceedingly well, which was surprising because her clothing was right out of the century before; turquoise on her neck, loose violet silk blouse, patterned full skirt—such a contrast with Ethel's curled hair, slacks, and lipstick.

I made strong, black coffee for my visitors. All that was lacking in old Navajo custom was cornhusk cigarettes which were long out of style but would have been smoked with esteem that day.

J. R. knew the tack I was taking on the mutilations, and mentioned it as soon as coffee had been served.

"Seen any new UFO's?"

I told him I hadn't, and his father said something in a sandstone voice. J. R. and his father conversed for awhile, a mortar of silence between each syllable and each gesture. Long silence. Talk. Silence again.

At last J. R. translated for me.

"My father says he saw something evil. A bunch of sheep killed the other day. He says it happened at night. My sister-in-law was supposed to be watching the sheep, but she went somewhere else for awhile and that's when they were killed."

"Any tracks?"

He raised the question of tracks to his father, who sat back in the chair and meditated. After a very long silence, the wavering voice filled the room.

"My father thinks it was dogs. No tracks. Fifteen sheep killed. He says he saw two white dogs, twice the size of normal dogs, on that night."

Navajo stories take their time to unravel.

"Were the bodies defiled?"

"What do you mean by defiled?"

"Were they mauled or bloodied?"

J. R. put it to his father, who shook his head sadly. It was obvious this pained the old man. The story could end here, like a box canyon with no way out.

Then he spoke again, keeping his eyes on J. R., away from me.

"My father says the sheep must not be moved until a certain

passage of time. Then they will be burned. That is the only way to discourage the evil."

"Was there a lot of blood, or was it like these mutilations I've read about and seen where there's none at all?"

"There was a lot of blood. A slaughter with nothing eaten."

"That doesn't make sense. Wild dogs, like any other predator, kill to eat, not to splash blood around."

"Maybe it wasn't dogs," J. R. said.

"Then what could it have been? Your father did say it was dogs, didn't he?"

Then J. R.'s father entered the conversation and his mother joined in. She leaned far forward in her chair, and I knew she would have been more at ease sitting on her haunches or on a flat stone before a fire. Neither the old man nor the old woman ever looked directly at me, but they were acutely aware of my presence. What they were now saying would determine whether I was going to learn much more or nothing more.

J. R. looked back in my direction.

"My father says this thing could have been anything at all."

I took a bold step, ready for failure.

"Skinwalkers?"

The word came out cold and hard. The old man knew that word of English even if he knew no other. Now he spoke forcefully to J. R.

"My father says it wasn't what you said. Says it could have been anything—mountain lion, maybe."

Another bold move, closer or further still from my goal: "I believe it was something else."

J. R. raised his eyebrows. The old man looked impassively at the ceiling.

"I think it was evil, but I would have to know more about it."

J. R. gave me a searching look. Was I the same man I once had been? This time when he turned to his father, his inflections were insistent. His father leaned forward with his elbows on the arms of his chair, assuming like his wife a sitting-by-the-campfire position. I felt he was trusting me for the first time, even though he refused to glance in my direction. He spoke to J. R. and his eyes were lit: he was saying something important.

They spoke together for what seemed like twenty minutes. I kept an attitude of quiet repose until they were finished. I did not want to give the impression of hanging on what was said.

"My father says to tell you that maybe it wasn't dogs, or if it was dogs, then they were commanded to do what they did by something."

I decided to avoid using that word that offended them and selected less volatile words.

"An evil intelligence?"

I saw the old man nod as I said it, though he nodded in J. R.'s direction, not mine, and said something else to him.

"My father says minds that can do these things are nowhere near when they are done. My father is blessed with the knowing of things that will happen in the future, and he told me that this would happen because of something that happened before it.

"There was a squaw dance last summer, and it was done in the enemy way to protect our family from harm. In the door of our house, I had found a bullet. No gun had been fired at that door, but there was the bullet buried in the wood. A bad thing was stalking the house, and we had to be aware. To exorcize the evil, we did the dance in the enemy way.

"We killed sheep for the dance, and their hides should have been destroyed. Instead, in a terrible mistake in ritual, my father sold the hides in town. Later, he said four lines had been drawn on the skins, four lines for the months that would pass before the evil could strike. In November, which is now, the bad things started to happen. My father got sick and almost died in the hospital. Earlier, he made a mistake when cleaning his rifle, fired a shot at my sister and nearly killed her. But the worst didn't happen to us, but to those fifteen sheep that died. The enemy way protected us. There are those on the reservation who fear us because of the things we have achieved, but my father has wisdom and they cannot hurt him."

"So you think the sheep were slain by agents of the evil that stalked your family—dogs or something else?"

134

"They don't have to lift a finger to accomplish their work."

"They never leave any tracks?"

J. R. asked his father, and the old man answered in swift, harsh Navajo. When he finished, J. R. himself was silent a long time. Then he faced his mother who said something to him. For a quick second, she looked at me and I saw that her handsome face was a clean and smooth as desert agate.

"They both say they have seen tracks. They say the tracks are this small."

He pinched his fingers to the size of a drinking glass, about five inches high.

"Like a child's," I said, astonished.

"Like a monkey's. Perfect little prints, like this."

Again, he made the size with his fingers. I felt a primordial fear that imaginary feet as small as a newborn infant's could be in the possession of a malign intelligence. I remembered well the first time I ever heard the story of the Navajo mother who had given birth to a baby perfect except for a mouth full of developed, canine teeth, hands covered with coarse hair, and feet toenailed like an ape.

"My father says he has seen the face of the thing—not wolflike at all. He says he has seen an ape-thing face looking down at him from the smoke hole of our summer hogan."

Indians have a way of talking about leaving for some time before they actually get moving. J. R.'s parents began speaking to him of departing, but they made no movements to leave. Then on command from the old man, each member of the family got to his feet. I knew our talk had gone as far as it could in translation. The old man said something to J. R. as we went out the door.

J. R. leaned toward me and whispered: "My father says the man who built a house in a hill is a good man."

I felt like an ambassador. "Thank your father and tell him I am honored to have both of your parents in my house."

J. R. said: "I think it would be easier to have my mother tell him that."

She did and he made a sound in his throat, then he got into the backseat of the pickup and hunched down until the only thing that could be seen was the big cowboy hat covering most of his face.

J. R.'s mother said one more sentence in Navajo as they prepared to drive off. J. R. lingered for a moment before getting into the driver's seat.

"She says you are invited to their wedding next week."

"Their wedding?"

"They were married according to Navajo custom fifty years ago to the day next Saturday. My older brother, who is a Christian, wants them to get married in a church in the Christian way."

"What does your mother say to that?"

"She doesn't care. She was raised in a mission school."

"And your father?"

"He doesn't care either. He's agreeable to it."

"Another fifty years are in the works," I said.

The old woman laughed, J. R. got into the truck, nodded good-bye, and drove down the hill with his family: six Navajos in a pickup watched over by the stargazer with a big cowboy hat in the backseat.

18

I had blood now. I was meeting the varmint, as Atkins liked to say. After months of indecision, I felt like I was on a path that was opening up.

I was curious whether the Pueblo Indians shared the skinwalker legend with the Navajos. Some reading on the subject revealed that, sure enough, the skinwalkers had walked east with the Navajo. They had come in all shapes and sizes: wolfmen, catmen, dogmen, foxmen, all of them wicked. The Pueblos, or course, also had the wise old trickster Coyote the Crazy to warn them and lead them to the edge of disaster.

It was important to understand that the animal gods were people and gods at once, earthly and immortal by turns. The foxmen and catmen of their evil underworld were not purely animal or purely human, but a combustible mixture.

Sadly enough, these days most Indians believed in their demons the same way they believed in their gods: half and half. Gods born in halves, end up in halves. Yet for some elders, like J. R.'s parents, the old ways were still the only ways.

I had to somehow find a crack in the Pueblo wall that would allow me to see into the old belief system. Unfortunately, the Pueblos guarded their secrets even more carefully than the Navajos.

My only hope was that a formal interview might yield more than obvious results. I chose a pueblo almost at my backdoor, but at a safer distance than Tesuque.

San Jacinto, located between Santa Fe and Picuris in the Rio Grande Valley, was typical of most New Mexican pueblos with its long line of sun-cracked, adobe houses and the old colonial Spanish church at the far end of the plaza.

I had been to San Jacinto before to witness their seasonal dances, and I knew that the governor's office was not far from the arts and crafts shop that sold fine silverwork.

I passed through a low portal and walked into a room that looked like a dentist's office. Imitation wood paneling covered the mud plaster. A young heavyset woman with doe eyes and a bad complexion, who was seated at a desk toward the center of the room, asked if I was the reporter who had called to see the governor. A door opened beside me and a short pueblo matron wheeled in a hospital cart that bore a feathered drum with a deerskin head.

"You may see the governor now," the secretary said. The governor, a round-faced man with thick, rimmed glasses and alert, black eyes, seemed no more at home in this office than the ceremonial drum had been in the reception room.

137

"I am Joe Juan Cello," he said, "acting governor of the pueblo."

I decided to get right to the point.

"The reason I'm here is to find out more about the cattle mutilations."

He looked a little perturbed, but he also seemed well-prepared.

"Should I repeat what I have already told the *New Mexican?*"

I had the feeling that nothing would come of the interview except direct questions and evasive answers, but if that were so, it didn't matter what I said.

"Maybe I've read too many books, but I believe there may be some witchcraft mixed into this thing."

"Indian legends are interesting to read. Most of them were written by white men who had an axe to grind."

"I admit that's true, but witches aren't confined to the pages of books. They're . . ."

"On broomsticks, no doubt."

"I'm talking about Navajo witches—skinwalkers."

His dark eyes lost their confident sparkle, and the certain smile that had been hidden behind his lips disappeared.

Suddenly I was on different ground with the man—dangerous ground.

"What do you know of such things?"

"I was a social worker at Window Rock before I took this job as a reporter."

"Well, a Navajo wolf wouldn't come this far east," he said with authority.

"That's a fact that has been troubling me from the start. I thought you might shed some light on it."

He gazed out the window at a cottonwood tree. A cluster of brown leaves hung from one of its branches, like a tight fist that refused to be shaken off by the wind. He looked tired of our conversation, and it hadn't even begun to go anywhere.

I knew I had played this about as far as it was going to go, so I stood up.

"Don't go yet," he said. "I want to tell you a story. It's about a friend of mine who liked to play jokes. One night we were out on the mesa, and a cow walked by us in the dark and scared us. My friend saw this as an excuse for one of his jokes. He had a .22 rifle all loaded up. Before I could stop him, he started shooting bullets into that cow, which turned out to be a half-grown calf.

"We were on pueblo land, but this cow belonged to a nearby rancher. My friend just poured bullets into it until it died. Do you know how many bullets you have to use to kill a calf with a .22? Maybe he put fifty shots into its head before it finally died. Then the two of us skinned the animal, cut up the meat, and took it back home with us.

"If anyone—like our parents—had caught us, we would have caught hell for sure, so we left big cuts of beef on the doorsteps of our best friends' houses. We knocked on the doors so the dogs wouldn't get the meat first. Then, when we were all done giving out the meat, my friend put that calfhide around his shoulders with the head wobbling on top of his and blood running down his face. He looked like the devil himself. Both of us were standing in the dark in front of an old man's house laughing when we felt something touch us on the shoulders.

"It was just a touch, but we both felt it. We both said 'What was that?' We turned around at the same time and the only thing there was the dark and the wind. My friend threw down that skin and we both ran home in a flash. To this day I haven't told anybody but you about that night. I'm telling you because you shouldn't mess with things you don't understand. We were kids—maybe that's an excuse and maybe it isn't—but the lesson is don't go places where you don't belong."

He was silent for a long time. The interview was over.

"Tell me something. Were you afraid of the cow's spirit, or something else?"

"We were afraid of the old man who lived in that house."

"Why?"

139

"Because people told us he was a wolf. We were doing something we shouldn't have done—I don't mean killing the cow, but putting the skin on. That was what was bad. Dangerous."

"You think someone in this pueblo is a skinwalker?"

"I'm not saying that." The invisible and invincible smile returned to his face.

That night I met Lorry in town at one of our favorite restaurants, a place with the unlikely name of Jimmie's Tiny's Lounge. Years earlier, it had been the after-hours hangout of the singers of the Santa Fe Opera, but now, especially during the off-season, it was where leather-faced Spanish-American men went to avoid their wives. We liked it. The food was simple and good and the atmosphere insured we could talk in privacy.

"I have a feeling," Lorry said, sipping a margarita from a glass heavily iced with salt, "that you are in another one of your blind funks. Am I right?"

"I don't know. This thing swings like a pendulum. I never get my equilibrium."

"What is the problem now? I bet you've had an experience you are not talking about."

"A couple, if you really want to know."

"I'm listening."

I watched across the room as an Indian couple entered. I'd seen these two all over Santa Fe, two losers who had been hard at booze since the day they graduated from the mission school. The man was a short, stocky fellow, wearing baggy, new, blue jeans rolled up at the ankles in 1940s style, tennis shoes salvaged from somebody's garbage, and a dime-store cowboy hat with drawstring under the chin. A bunch of Genghis Khan hairs sprouted from his upper lip and his mouth was full of missing teeth. His wife or booze-buddy or whatever she was kept ten paces in back of him. She dressed the same way with the notable substitution of an enormous floppy hat like you win at a carnival. The man ignored the persistent presence of the bedraggled woman, who always kept up a steady flow of Tewa banter.

"That's what's bothering me right there," I said under my breath.

"Them? What on earth do you mean?"

"This Indian crap depresses the hell out of me. I can take any amount of Spanish degradation, but I like my Indians on the holy side."

"Well, you haven't had to interview those two, have you? Anyway, it's not like you have never seen such things. This is welfare land, remember? Fourth generation handout country. I don't see what drunk Indians have to do with your feeling depressed again about your work."

"Nothing really, except that sometimes it gets me down: evil and drunkenness and flies and corpses and drums that come at you on hospital carts. If something sacred has occurred, I don't know what it is. All these wheezy boozers coming into my office."

"You've only had one of those from what you've told me, and he helped you."

"Yeah, I've got no complaints. Hey, you usually get your back up when I'm feeling like this."

"I know, but I don't want to contend with any more depression or your wanting to quit the *Review*."

"Who said anything about quitting. I just pointed out that I was tired of it all."

"Why don't you go to the dances tonight. That always cheers you up."

"I feel like leaving the Indians to themselves. Shit, here I am prying their secrets out of their fists. I'm no better than the next person who tries to steal something from them."

"The difference is that they respect you, Gerry. How do you think you get stories, anyway—not by being an ass. They trust you."

"Then I break that trust by writing some blood and guts stuff for the *Review*."

"Your healing piece was beautiful. Everyone said so. I sent a copy to Mom and she liked it, too."

"That's all I need to hear right now, but thanks for the encouragement."

"What I don't understand is why these things get you down all of a sudden. You're going along fine, then zonko you're lying on the ground."

"There's stuff you don't know about. I haven't wanted to worry you."

"You told me all about that weird automatic writing. I didn't think you were that disturbed by it. After all, you've written a whole book of poems by that method."

"They were my words, my sentences. This was somebody else talking. That Etienne, I don't know about him."

"So you think Etienne put thoughts in your head?"

"I don't know anymore. One day Etienne seems innocent, another day he doesn't."

"I know his wife. The only thing about Etienne that she says is a little hard to fathom is that he has had a bunch of out-of-body experiences. He wanders around out of his body while he's sound asleep in bed with her."

"Did she tell you that he has tapes of extraterrestrials talking to him from outer space?"

"No, she didn't. That sounds a bit . . ."

"Yeah, doesn't it. I like the guy. I just don't know where he's coming from."

"You said you were planning a trip north with him to interview Indians. Do you think he's the right companion for a trip to unfamiliar country?"

"He's either harmless or completely wacky. In either case, yes, I have made some tentative plans with him to go interview Gomez and maybe a few other people."

"Why do you have to take him along if you don't know whether you trust him? Doesn't sound like you."

"He has a way of getting things out of people with his off-the-wall questions."

142

The Indian couple, having been refused a drink, had gotten into a big argument with the bartender. With a brisk elbow clutch that suggested many years of practice, he showed them the door.

The cold night air invaded the bar. Outside, the two Indians were discussing their next bar hop. His Tewa curses and her denials faded and the bar went back to being a gracious den of darkness.

"What do they do on a night like this?" Lorry asked.

"Where do they sleep, you mean? They'll probably hitch home to Tesuque Pueblo and sleep in their own soft beds. Get up and head out in the morning. Same ageless ceremony."

"That is a ceremony I'd like to indulge in myself right about now."

"Alright," I said, "let's blow this joint."

Only after we got back home did I remember the significance of the dances I was going to miss over at San Jacinto. This was the night of the animal dances. Out of the *kiva* they came, horned and shaggy maned, the stamping men and light-stepping women. It only happened once a year, and I knew that I ought not to miss it, not because it had anything to do with assignments or research, but because I liked to go every year. The rich symbolic meaning in the animal dances was as palpable as the night wind's message of the coming snows. They could and often did bring down the snows that melted into green willow-water in the spring. Without the mountain runoff, the crops would wither in the summer sun. So the dances were really prayers for hopeful crops, for good yearly blessings, for all sentient life at the pueblo. The dances warded off evil and celebrated all that was good and regenerative. I wanted to see the men-animals move in a rhythm older than time, and forget Jimmie's Tiny's forlorn children of the night.

19

The pueblo was hushed when I arrived. The Indians stood in groups wearing heavy coats with Pendleton blankets thrown over their shoulders. Some of them wore beaded mocassins, but most wore the low-cut, squaw boots with silver *conchos* on the side. The squat women had blankets raised over their heads, and their round faces were lit up by the moon. Even the mongrel dogs succumbed to the silence by lying down in the cold dust. The children either were held on their mothers' hips or they stood beside them.

As my eyes grew accustomed to the night shapes, I saw tepee fires prepared all over the plaza. There must have been a hundred of them, stretching as far as the church, a great-shouldered shape that seemed out of place until I saw that a torch-lit procession was emerging from its huge wooden doors.

At a somber pace, thirty or forty Indians formed a procession led by a Catholic priest and followed by a man who fired a rifle every ten or fifteen steps. The blasts echoed in the adobe plaza. The procession snaked around the old cottonwood in the center of the plaza, then turned east. An Indian with a torch came out of the dark and began to light the cones of piñon wood.

I moved out of the shadows and joined a group of Indians who stood in a circle around one of the fires. They greeted me with courteous nods and enlarged their circle to include me.

In time, as we waited for the dancers to emerge from the kiva, the Indians in our circle moved to other ones. After an hour's wait, around the dwindling fire were only myself, a man, and a woman. "You from Los Alamos?" the man asked.

"I live in Tesuque."

"Not such a long ways away."

"You got a wife and children?" said the woman.

"Yes."

"Bring your whole family next time. Children love dancing."

"Wonder when the dancers gonna come out now?" the man said.

"Soon. They come soon," said the woman. As she spoke, a puff of snowflakes came out of the sky. In a moment the whole plaza was white. Then laughter and excited voices rose from the clusters around the fires. The dancers had come out of the kiva at last.

First came the rows of buffalo-headed men with black chests that heaved when they stepped with a rush of bells and gourd rattles. A deerskin drum thumped steadily as more and more dancers appeared out of the clouds of new snow. Then the deer-dancers moved toward us. Their hands gripped sticks to prod the earth exactly like deer hooves. As they did their stiff-legged dance, they emitted cries that sounded like knife slashes in the dark. On the tips of their heavy antlers was eagle down, thought to be an intimation of snowflakes.

Straight-backed pueblo women held sprigs of evergreen as they stepped lightly from side to side. Dressed up as antelopes, children sported about with white bobs of tail and two-pronged heads.

When the animal dancers began to file back into the kiva, the snow (almost on command) tapered off. The Indians who had gathered around the piñon fires started to move toward the parking lot. The engines of pickup trucks coughed on in the cold air, and headlights dispelled the lingering magic of the dance.

Reluctantly, I headed toward my car. A small figure was waiting intently in the dim shadows. Right away I recognized the round face and darting eyes of Joe Juan Cello, the governor.

"Something has happened that you might want to take a look at."

I followed him to a pueblo police car and we drove toward the fields that lay below the plaza. The moon was out now, and the snow on the meadow grass shone. The driver cut his headlights, and the car traveled quietly through the open fields.

The car stopped in front of the huge carcass of a steer, tilted on its side. Its head was arched upward as if the neck had been snapped.

145

"Just like the last one," Joe Juan Cello said. "Look here."

He and the uniformed Indian driver squatted by the cow's head. "No sign of blood anywhere."

I leaned forward to look into the steer's open mouth. The absence of a tongue made the mouth unbearably wicked, like the steer was laughing at us. The lips had been removed, so the teeth looked like those of a *tyrannosaurus rex*, not a gentle vegetarian.

The tribal officer moved to the back of the steer. "No balls," he said. "Been cut off." This incision was so clean it appeared to have always been there. The officer got down on his knees and sniffed the fur. "There's that smell again, Joe," he said. "That burned smell." An odor of singed hair hung around the animal.

"Same old story," Joe Juan Cello sighed. "No blood, no tracks, no tongue, no balls."

"What about that smell?" I asked.

"They smell like that," the officer said. "Every one of them."

"Sandia Labs doesn't know what to make of it," added the governor. "They do a radiation check, but so far nothing's come of it."

"May I borrow your flashlight?" I asked the officer.

He handed me a flashlight with a foot and a half long handle. Neither of them had bothered to use the light up close. I beamed it at the cow's mouth, from which a wisp of steam was coming. Then I shone it around various places on the body and handed the light back to the officer, who quickly snapped it off.

"We don't want the pueblo to know about this one," Joe Juan Cello said. "It would spoil the dances. Well, have you gotten any clues?"

"Not a single one."

"Some mutilations are uglier than this one. They're getting it down alright. Getting it to the point where one night there'll be a man lying here instead of a cow. What'll the state cops say then? What would they say if one of their boys was lying here without any balls?"

"They'd be pissed," I said. "You can count on that."

"Well, right now they're not pissed. They're just curious."

146

Then I looked beyond the surgery and saw, for the first time, the cow as a whole. Its head was too big for the rest of its body and seemed disconnected at the neck. The midsection had fallen in on the ribs, as if the cow had been starved to death. I would see its broken-necked, laughing-teethed mockery in my sleep for the next couple of nights. I wanted to get away from the burned stink of dead cow and return to the pine smell of dance fires.

From the car driving back to the village, I noticed that the rest of the San Jacinto herd had gathered under a cottonwood, shoulder to shoulder. An intense wall of animal eyes followed us into the darkness.

The dances had picked me up, but the mutilation had dropped me right back down where I had been before I had left that bar with Lorry. I kept seeing the eyes of those cattle all the way home; what they knew and what we couldn't know was festering in my mind. The first symptoms of an allergic reaction to mutes were making my insides itch.

I turned off State Road 22 down our driveway. The dirt road was so steep you had to be careful your forehead didn't bump up against the dashboard of your car. The road dipped into the arroyo lined with sage and chamisa and came up on the other side; two more winds and turns and I was heading up the last slope to the house, which in the moonlight looked like a magnificent white mushroom. A dust of new snow lay everywhere.

I undressed in the dark so I wouldn't wake Lorry, but the moment I slid under the covers, she sat bolt upright, her body a coiled spring of nerves. She flung her arms around my neck in a life-and-death grip.

"Hey, you're crushing my neck. Take it easy." Her strength was amazing. "Did you have a bad dream or something?"

"I'm scared," she whispered.

"You are terrified. What's the matter?"

I felt warm tears on my cheek. She wouldn't let go of my neck.

Through the window, pale slabs of moon silvered the floor. The night was still, like the pueblo before the lighting of the torches.

"Are the kids alright?"

147

"I'm afraid to look. Go check the children's room."

I shot out of bed pulling on my pants and went down the hall into their room. Two warm bodies were safe under the rumpled pink comforter of their big double bed. I felt their foreheads for a fever—Lorry sometimes got out of control when they were running fevers—but they both felt tranquil and cool. For a moment I listened to the sweet music of their quiet breathing. Nothing seemed out of place.

Back in the bedroom Lorry was standing in her nightgown, looking like a redhaired moon princess.

"Do you hear it?" she asked ominously, her head cocked to the side.

"Probably another asshole up the arroyo."

"It's a hurt animal. I've been listening to it ever since you left for the dances."

"What kind of animal?"

Her face was all raw-boned tension, like a half-drowned cat.

"Oh, Lorry, I don't like to see you this frightened. Will you please tell me what kind of thing is out there this time, and I'll go out and deal with it."

"I'm not hearing things," she pouted.

Then I heard a clear high-pitched scream.

I rushed to the window. Dressed in cactus and snow sparkles, the desert looked unreal.

"You've been hearing that since I left?"

"Yes. Ever since the kids went to bed. Thank God it hasn't gotten them up."

"Sounds like an owl to me."

"Owls that scream are in nightmares."

."No, they're in real life, too. Barred owls make every kind of sound in the book: hiss, wail, shriek, moan, cough. They can sound like a bitch dog in heat. One little owl can make all that noise. I've heard them on camping trips, and always at the lake as a child."

"This isn't the lake and you're not a child. I've been listening to that thing for hours, and I'm telling you it isn't any owl."

"Shut up for a second, will you? I just heard it again."

"Now maybe you'll . . ."

At the window was the unmistakable hiss of a snake about to strike, and then we both heard glass crashing.

Something heavy thumped to the floor. The hissing continued, and now there was a new sound: something sidewinding across the thick, dry hemp of the carpet.

"Don't move a goddamned inch," I said. "We've got a snake in the room. Someone just broke the window and heaved a snake in here."

Lorry stood still. I trained my eyes at the floor. Slowly, with much precision, I slipped my belt through the loops of my Levis. Holding my buckle, I let the belt hang loosely on the floor.

"You said not to move," Lorry said. "What are you doing with that belt."

I spoke so softly I could hardly hear myself talk.

"Better for it to bite a belt than a leg."

We listened for the slithering of scales on the rough hemp. Then the room was filled with buzzing rattles.

"It's taken its position," I whispered hoarsely.

"Now what do we do?"

"We don't move. Where do you think it's coming from?"

"It's by the bed," she said, "I see it now. Gerry, please get it out of here before it gets into the children's room. Kill it. Please kill it."

"I'm looking. I don't see anything. Where do you see it?"

"By the covers there. It's lying on the coverlet that fell off the bed."

The moon lit the room, but I could see no snake. There was something dark by the right side of the bed. Cautiously, I made my way toward it, holding the belt in front of me. As I got closer, the buzzing increased. The rattle changed to the sound of a dry gourd. Suddenly, I beat at the floor with the belt. I was swinging that belt like John Henry when Lorry grabbed my wrist in her steel grip.

"It's gone," she said faintly.

"Gone? How could that be?"

"I felt it leave the room. It's gone from the house. Look at the floor."

By the coverlet was a brown sock. I had been attacking the sock I had taken off my own foot when I first got into bed. The room was quiet. I turned around to inspect the smashed window. There wasn't a crack in it. I gazed out at the snow-pure night. What was going on?

"You shouldn't have beaten it so," Lorry said almost inaudibly.

"You told me to get it out. You ordered me to do it. So I get the thing the hell out, and now you're mad at me because I did it too rough. A snake's a snake, Lorry. You don't play with snakes."

"There was no snake."

"What do you mean, no snake?"

"We have both had a bad dream. There is no broken window, no snake. I think we have gone off the deep end."

I kept staring in disbelief at that windowpane. I had heard the sprinkling of glass filaments, the spray of fragments. The sound of that snake was not something I was going to get talked out of—the snake was real. Even though I had not seen it, I had heard it.

Lorry looked small in the moonlight. A princess no longer, she was a withered child. I felt like using the belt on her backside. She was responsible for whatever it had been. Before I could think clearly, I heard the children. Mariah was standing there in the bedroom.

"Daddy," she said, "what was all that noise?"

"No noise," I answered firmly. "It was the ants again. Remember those ants that got into the ceiling last summer? Well, they're back again. I was getting them out of our bed."

"Were you beating them with your belt?" she asked innocently.

"I was using my belt for something else."

"You were hitting Mommy. See, she's crying."

"Let's all go back to bed," Lorry sobbed. Hannah came into the room, rubbing her eyes. "I heard a big cat that was hissing."

"It's gone now," Lorry said in a surer tone. "All of us were having a horrible dream." Now she was in control again. Good, we were going to need a lot of control. I felt that I had less control than Hannah.

"I wasn't having a bad dream," Mariah reasoned.

"Yes, you were." I swore stupidly.

"I wasn't dreaming and I didn't dream about any cat hissing, and now I'll never get back to sleep again because you were lying about those ants and you were really hitting Mommy with that belt."

"I was not hitting Mommy with my belt, I was . . ."

"We're all beginning to sound like babies," Lorry said. "I think we should all get into bed together and go to sleep like one big happy family."

Instantly, Hannah hopped into our bed. She loved family sleepathons. "I like Mommy and Daddy's bed," she giggled.

"I don't want to go to sleep with bad Daddy," Mariah scowled.

"I'm going downstairs and make some hot chocolate," I said.

"Me too, Da," Hannah piped. She was really into an all-night thing. A party suited her fine.

Lorry told Mariah that I had only thought there were ants in the bed, and that I hadn't touched her with the belt. Everything was really alright, and the only reason she had been crying was because she had stubbed her big toe getting out of the way of the ants that weren't really there. Mariah seemed to accept this last line of bull by suspension of disbelief, and we headed downstairs for the kitchen.

I lit a blaze of a fire in the fireplace while Lorry put milk on the stove. I turned on the radio to add to the festivities, a good country station came in loud and clear from Tulsa. The first song was Hoyt Axton singing about rusty old haloes and angels with busted luck. We all sipped at the hot chocolate and burned our tongues, listening to country music and getting over a bad scare.

Then Lorry turned the radio down low and read to Hannah and Mariah from a sweet and easy storybook. Both of them conked out in Lorry's lap in no time at all. We stowed them back in their bed and came downstairs again to talk. The night had been too much for Lorry, for while I made another draft of hot chocolate she too conked out, right on the kitchen table, head on her arms. I sat down and considered what had happened.

Had there been a snake? A broken window? Had there been two

crazy people thrashing out their fears in the middle of the night? Was it one and not the other, or were they both equally crazy? Did each support the other's fear? The only thing I couldn't write off was that hissing and buzzing, and the dead weight falling of those sinuous coils of snake. I realized that only the sounds were real. There had been no physical evidence of their causes.

With a jarring clangor, the phone rang, and rang, and rang. I was frozen to my seat. Lorry woke with a start.

"The phone is ringing," she said as if she were wide awake.

"I'll get it. Stay where you are."

I recognized the caller immediately as the Frenchman Etienne Renaldier.

"Have you need of anyone?" the voice intoned like a priest.

It was one of the few times in my life that I was actually speechless. Lorry seemed to understand my predicament.

"Who is it?"

I cupped the phone with my hand. "That Etienne guy. I don't want to talk to him."

"Let me have the phone then." She grasped it like a true-blue secretary and began speaking to him.

"No everything is alright, now," I heard her say. "You did? I'll tell him. That's so good of you. When? Now, did you say now? Well, I don't know if it is alright with us. Now is a pretty weird time of the morning. We were just about to go to bed. Oh, you do? I see, well, I guess it's alright. We'll be waiting, then. Good-bye."

"Don't tell me you invited that nutty Frenchy over here for hot chocolate. For Christ's sake, Lorry, it's four in the morning."

"I know what time it is. He was insistent. I was just too tired to argue with the man. What's the difference? It's almost time to get up anyway."

"The difference is that he is not welcome at this hour."

"Why didn't you tell him that yourself?"

"I don't know."

"Well, I don't know why I didn't tell him to shove it, either."

"Makes sense. What'd he want?"

152

"He said he had something important to tell you about what happened tonight."

"What does he know about what happened?"

"I have no idea, but he knew."

"I want plenty of coffee."

"I'm going to make a couple of gallons, strong enough to float a horseshoe."

"I want to go outside for a minute and get a breath of fresh air."

"It'll be ready in a few minutes. Don't go away now."

"No, I'm just going to lean against the front door and breathe some air."

I sucked the cold air down to my toes. The sky was a frozen pewter gray. With deep intakes of fresh air, my drugged feeling was subsiding.

A car chugged around the turns of our windy narrow road. Either Etienne had made it out in record time, or I had lost track of time again.

In another moment, a blue Volvo puffed up the hill to our house. He waved with a most cheerful, friendly expression. I wondered if I could converse with anyone that merry so early in the morning after a totally sleepless night.

He popped out of the car like an inflatable doll. He was wearing at least ten ski sweaters. His arms stuck out like sticks.

"You look cold," he said when he came up to me.

"You look a little overdressed yourself."

Lorry opened the front door. "Coffee is ready." She seemed pleased to have this little diversion.

The table was set with clean coffee cups. A coffee cake, one of those frozen kind you heat-up, graced the table. She looked cheerful. I started to feel more normal.

"My God," I said, "I feel like I'm just coming down from a pretty bad high."

Etienne threw back his head and laughed. He began to pull himself out of the sweaters.

Lorry seemed fine. I was still a bit out of it.

"How do you feel now?" Etienne asked. "Better?"

As he said it, I did begin to feel more at ease.

"I'm better now." Saying it, I felt better still.

"Tell me, Etienne," I said as I sipped some hot coffee. "Do you believe in trances?"

His eyebrows knitted like an old lady's. "Of course I believe! I have been in and out of trances all my life."

"Do you believe in witches?"

This tickled him so much that he almost spilled his coffee on the sweater currently on the outside.

"Noo, no, no, nooo. I do believe in powers that harm, and you must guard yourself against them. But witches, I don't believe in them. They are only in children's books."

"Someone else said that same thing to me tonight."

"You mean last night," he said. "Look, the sun is up already."

He said it with great expectancy, and we went to the window to see the blood light break from a cleft in the upper canyon.

"The sun is good. You were saying that someone said something to you last evening."

"Yes, but before I tell you about it, let me ask you this: how did you know that something was wrong out here?"

"Easy."

"How?" I insisted.

"I know when my friends are in trouble. I cannot tell you how I know. It is something that has been given to me. My healer, the Philippino doctor, saw it in my aura. I have always known it was there. I felt something very bad was about to happen the night of the mutilation at San Reymo. So I called you."

"We didn't know each other then. So why did you call me?"

"I have already explained why it was you. You were in sympathy with us."

"Who's us?" Lorry asked.

Etienne let out his bubbly laugh, spilled his coffee on a turtleneck. "I don't mean anything by *us*. I meant to say *me*."

"What do you mean by 'in sympathy'?" I said.

154

"I told you at San Reymo. Listen, you two should trust me by now, because I am your friend. I came here to help you. I had bad fears for you on this night. Can you tell me what was here? I know that something was threatening both of you."

"It was a cat," I said simply. "We had a wildcat in our house. We found it, chased it, and got it out the door."

"A wildcat? In your home?"

"Yup. It must've come in through the open window, upstairs."

"I had the window open while I was cooking," Lorry hastened to add. It was a necessary, good lie. We had always worked together to protect ourselves from the rest of the world.

"I had a feeling it was not a real animal," Etienne said, looking at each of us over the edge of his coffee cup.

"However, I believe you, if you say that it was."

"Suppose we only heard it, only *thought* we saw this cat. What would you say to that?" I asked.

"I would probably say that that is closer to what I felt. You were telling me before that someone had said something to you last evening. Who was it?"

"The governor at the pueblo. He told me about skinwalkers, the wolfmen or witches in Indian belief."

"I know them. This was why you asked me about witches, wasn't it?"

"Yes."

"Was this governor a witch? In your mind, did he seem like one?"

"The thought crossed my mind, but then a moment ago, I must confess . . ."

"Ah, ha, the truth comes out," he laughed. "Do you still think I am one myself? I know when you are in trouble—does that make me a witch?"

"The thought crossed my mind."

Lorry got up from the table and began to clear the cups and saucers. No one had touched the coffee cake.

"I want to go to bed," she said. "Etienne, will you excuse us?

We are very tired. I don't think I can keep awake much longer."

"No problem. I will go now. I would not have disturbed you except that I was worried."

He stretched out his hand and offered me a gift. "Please wear this." In his hand was an ancient silver cross, black with age.

"What kind is it?" I said.

He could see that I was suspicious of it.

"Coptic. It was found fifteen hundred years ago in a tomb in Greece. It will protect you, if you help protect yourself. Wear it with my blessing."

"What religion do you belong to?" Lorry said abruptly, standing at the other end of the room by the sink.

"Me? I am a member of the Christian Brotherhood. The Philippino doctor is one, Harjac another. There are many of us in town. We don't publicize our gatherings, we have no church, but we recognize one another. We practice only good, not evil. You must not worry about me getting close to you—I feel you are both afraid, not of me, but of anyone getting too close to your family. You must protect yourself, Gerry. You are too close to the things that we are trying to destroy. Be careful. Go with God."

He was most serious. He had named my feeling about his coming into the house at such an unpredictable time: fear, only fear.

"Do you believe the cat was real, Etienne?" Lorry asked.

"Are you sure it was a cat?"

"Without question."

"Do not give in to anything that does not go with God," he said. "Go with light and you will be protected. The cross will help."

"Why didn't you give that cross to Lorry? She was the one who saw the cat first."

"You brought it into the house, Gerry. It was on you even before you came in the door."

"I brought it in?"

"Yes, quite innocently of course. You got it at the pueblo. This is what I believe anyway. If I tell you more I will increase its chances of coming back. Get rid of that smell on you and your clothes by

156

thinking good thoughts. Stay out of the thoughts of those who wish you harm. Gerry, it is you who are walking with skins. Believe me when I say it. Well I have to go now. Mei will be worried when she sees I am not in bed with her. Remember to wear the cross."

After he was gone, I dropped the cross in my sock drawer for good. I dreaded the crusted black on the ancient metal.

"He means well. I think he does, anyway," Lorry said.

"That Christian Brotherhood talk gave me the creeps."

"He was wrong, you know."

"About what?"

"You were nowhere near this house when I first heard the hissing outside the window. We will have to think of what to do after we get some rest. I am too tired to think about any of it."

"I'm not quitting this assignment. I'm hooked."

"Come to bed and we'll get hooked together."

"I'm not quitting. I'm going to finish the articles, every last one of them."

"Bring your articles to bed, too," she said.

"That is the second time someone has given me a cross. Do you remember the natural stone one given me by Bart up in Taos? He said it would protect me, just like Etienne."

"Bring the stone cross to bed, too, if you want. Just come to bed, will you?"

Part Four

The Warning

20

Above Abiquiu on the road to Chama and Pagosa Springs, the landscape of sculptured rock changed dramatically to sagebrush and pine bordered by snow peaks. The road wound past towns of wood and mud with red tin roofs. The muddy Chama River slammed down from the ice mountains and spilled over its banks into tributaries lined with young red and green willow and into the new irrigation ditches. Occasionally, the skin of a coyote hung on a Spanish barb fence to ward off other predators.

The time had finally come to meet Angel Gomez on his turf. I was traveling with Etienne to Dulce, the Jicarilla Apache Reservation, where the state policeman had his remote headquarters. It was up in high mountain country, rolling with blue sage, muddy ponies, and the empty-engined hulks of '52 Chevies. We came into Dulce late in the day. Government housing and cinder block and dull brick establishments composed the town.

"Is this the state police headquarters?" I asked a fat Apache hosing down a tribal police car in front of a drab building surrounded by government automobiles.

"Supposed to be."

Inside were a kicked-in Planter's peanut machine and a dispatcher behind a glass window. Wearing a huge brimmed, black cowboy hat, complete with eagle feather, the dispatcher was speaking Apache into a C.B.

"We're looking for Angel Gomez," I said through the hole in the window.

"He's on his way. You from ABC news?"

"No, but we have an appointment to see him."

"He'll be here in a couple of minutes."

We sat on the tailgate of my Subaru station wagon and ate chicken salad sandwiches. I rehearsed the questions I knew I'd forget when I met Angel Gomez in his own digs. Earlier in the week, the *National Enquirer* had run a photo he had taken of a UFO with some of his remarks and theories. Since then, he had been interviewed at least a hundred times. I wanted to interview him not because of all the media attention, but because of the frequency of mute events in his sector.

In 1977, Gomez had been named policeman of the year for getting the drop on a convicted murderer who had escaped from maximum security at the state penitentiary in Cerrillos, New Mexico. For over a year, the escapee had evaded capture, leaving messages in Spanish to taunt Gomez whenever the officer spent the night in a mountain village—sleeping on a spare cot or a corn crib—or in his car.

"Sooner or later, I will have him," he told newspapers only weeks before he played gas station attendant in an inbred Spanish town famous for shootings, slayings, and burnings. In Chorasco, if a man coveted his neighbor's house or his wife, he took them. If by burning his neighbor's house, he got neither the wife nor domocile, he nonetheless got the pleasure of seeing a house burn in the night.

That day in February 1977, he poured a half-tank of gas into his quarry's beat-up Ford and observed the .38 on the front seat. As he wiped bugs off the cracked windshield, he pulled his own revolver and laid it smoothly against the head of the outraged, yet helpless man who, when he had recovered from his amazement, stupidly grabbed *his* .38 and pointed it through the windshield at Gomez's right earlobe. Gomez cocked his weapon and his triumphant grin said, "Alright then, let's blow each other straight to hell."

The other man cocked his .38 with the same confident smile and they both stared at each other while the sweat rolled down their foreheads, down their necks, and into their underwear. They were both found at that same standoff when reinforcements showed up and finally talked the prisoner into surrender, his smile by then gone dim in defeat.

So it was no surprise to me when Gomez got the drop on *us* as we were eating. He came up quietly in his tight, dark blue uniform. He knew exactly who we were this time before we introduced ourselves. After a few static-filled calls on his radio, he drove us to the Little Beaver Coffee Shop.

"How about a cup of coffee before we see the latest in cut-up cows?"

"You mean there has been another recent one we don't know about?"

"The story isn't out yet. First we got to do a chemical check to see if the blood's been coagulated. After that we tell the taxpayers what we think."

Inside the cafe the usual soft-spoken, red-faced cowboys hunkered around Formica tables over their third or fourth cup. The place was run by fat squaws with narrow wolf eyes.

Gomez waved for coffee, made a remark to the one man behind the counter, a sallow, thin-shouldered fellow with fine, braided hair and a bright eagle plume tied into the side of his head. He looked authentic, but there was something curiously effeminate in his stance. When Gomez teased him in Spanish, he shook his head and smiled back like a girl.

Gomez reminded me once more of Brando around the time of

163

One-Eyed Jacks; tough, good-looking, and a country boy all at the same time. A flick of his wrist and the refills came, one cup after another.

"There's a lot of this air turbulence talk," he said. "Sticks and branches and stuff blown all around, but we can't prove nothing up here in Dulce."

"Why's that?"

"Simple. Look out that window, what'd you see? Not a god-damn thing but sagebrush. In Wolverton, Montana, where there's been a bunch of mutilations, the ground shows turbulence. Down in Lamy, New Mexico, we did a turbulence test with a helicopter, and it blew sand all over hell. Up here in Dulce, there's just no way of telling what kind of aircraft's being used.

"You've said many times in the newspapers that there are UFOs here. Do you still maintain they exist?" Etienne asked.

"Well," he said, slicking his hair back with his open palm, "*if* you call it proof. I say one thing one time, and another another time, because that's what I believe at that time when I make a statement. Later, I change my mind. So what is this proof? Okay, I'll tell you, or you can read that *National Enquirer* article with my picture in it."

A squaw came from behind the counter and dutifully pressed a newspaper into Gomez's hand.

"Here's a picture of something I never saw, but it showed up afterwards. The infrared in the camera caught these balloons, or puffs of smoke, or flying saucers, or airborne mushrooms, or whatever in hell they're supposed to be."

"Apache smoke signals," said one of the cowboys, pretending not to be listening. The two loungers drinking coffee with him burst into laughter.

The photo showed two round shapes like darkened thumbprints at the far corner of the sky. The picture was taken in broad daylight.

"Who knows what they are," Gomez said. "They're what you want them to be, I guess."

"Then what makes you say last week you have seen a UFO?" Etienne asked.

"Parlez vooze Francez?" Gomez asked back.

"Of course." Etienne was more bored than embarrassed by the smiles across the room.

"What I saw a week ago was an aircraft moving low in the sky with a big white floodlight. It could've been a UFO, or maybe something else. It was shaped like a round bubble and made no noise. There were no lights on the thing except that floodlight. When they—or whatever was in it—turned off the big light, you couldn't see a thing because it was pitch black out. If I'd had my AR–16, I would've blown the sonofabitch right outta the sky."

"You would kill them for flying over your head?"

"I'd blow the bastards to hell just for the proof," he swaggered and then continued, "Look, guys, there's an explanation for everything. I respect people like Dr. Sigmund who think it's UFOs. I've looked at his pictures, and I think they're real. Sometimes I think I have the answers, other times I just get confused. Right now it seems to me they're going for the intake and outtake mechanisms of a plain old cow for one reason. They take bone marrow from the pelvis, they take the lymphatic node, they take the *chingado*, the tongue, the tissue around the face, and the cow's blood. Whoever or whatever's doing this is looking for something in that animal that will show up only in those areas of its body. They take the eye—why the eye? Because everything that animal eats shows up in its eye. What I think is maybe the government lost something in the atmosphere, and they're taking preventative measures to see no more human beings get killed because of it."

"You must be talking about germ warfare," I said.

"Yes, I am. I think this UFO business could be another big government cover-up for something much worse than little green men in flying saucers. Those little green men—who knows—just might be friendly. Germs are a different story." Gomez waved for his sixth cup of coffee.

"You would kill these little green men, even if they are making no aggression towards you?" said Etienne.

Gomez laughed. "They must love spaceships in France," he

remarked to me. "What is this, a religion with you?" he asked Etienne.

"In fact, it is. I believe that we may have these visitors because of what you say about the germ warfare."

"Yes," I added, "the star people may want the same facts you think the government's after."

"I don't say anything's impossible anymore. I'll tell you what I'm waiting for right now—a lab report from London. They just had a cattle mutilation over there. Blood removed through the jugular vein with a blowing and sucking machine. There are indications of the same anticoagulant that we've been picking up over here."

"How does that show up in the mutilation?"

"Pink blood, bright pink. Spots all around on the ground, and, of course, in the animal itself. I'll tell you another thing makes me think these things are government jobs, maybe worldwide political cover-ups. There's something in the air that could harm us, but they're not saying what it is. Our national security people don't give a damn or they would've listened to my lab reports two years ago. A lot of anthrax has been showing up in these cattle that get mutilated. That's classified, so keep it to yourself. The last thing we want in New Mexico is an anthrax scare, but it keeps showing up again and again, and no one in Washington cares."

"Why do you think there have been so many mutilations up here in Dulce?"

Gomez gave me his broadest grin. "You haven't done your homework, have you? Better go back and read the papers. In 1967 there was that thing they called Gas Buggy. The government exploded a 2717-megaton bomb just twelve miles from here. The Atomic Energy Commission was trying to open a natural gas shelf formation or whatever they call it, and they spent thirty-three million bucks. What'd they get? High radiation in all the wells. Indians got hit the worst. Hey, Gray Eagle, how come you guys always get it up the *culo*?"

The slim, ladylike Apache came out from behind the counter. While pouring Gomez's seventh cup of coffee, he said in an easy voice: "We have always given white people the benefit of the doubt. Why not? They are crazy."

21

Our plan was to rest up after the long drive and the interview with Gomez, and hit him with another bunch of questions in the morning.

We took a small cabin just outside of town beside a creek. The snow-water crashing down from the higher elevations near the Colorado border was so loud it kept us awake. We made coffee on a hot plate and ate a couple more of the sandwiches Etienne's wife had made. They were filled with the best chicken salad I had ever eaten, full of secret spices.

"Your wife can make sandwiches better than anyone in the western world," I joked.

"That's because she's from the eastern world," he said, an uneven elfin smile on his lips. None of his teeth seemed to match, but none of the rest of him did either.

"Where is Mei from, anyway?" I asked.

"Detroit. She is Japanese, of course, but more American than you are, I think. Her parents were in camps in this country during the war, but it had no effect on her except to make her more aware of food than other people. Mei can make a hot dog into a banquet."

"How long have you been married?"

"About three years. Our Akido master married us in Santa Fe. I took a Japanese name from him, Kimito, which I have since abandoned in favor of my chosen name, Etienne."

I looked out the calico curtain at the sundown creeping into the red willows on the river banks. Great tendrils of ice had come loose from these willows in the sun and were being batted about by the stiff current.

"This country around here," Etienne said, "reminds me of the place where my father had a chalet in Switzerland. I used to go there often when I was a boy."

I took a good look at Etienne. I had known him for weeks, I had been to his house, met his wife, played with his little girl and had now come six hundred miles into desolate mountains on a common quest, and yet I felt I did not know him at all. There was nothing secretive about the man, yet some part of him lurked in the dark, unknown to even himself. Come to think of it, I wasn't really sure why Etienne was with me at all. He was not earning money by doing interviews, which was my rationale; otherwise I would be at home in front of a crackling fire reading Wallace Stevens. He had brought enough sandwiches to last two full days—that's a lot of chicken salad—and had blithely paid for the gas. I trusted him, at least I thought I did. Lorry thought going on this trip with him was a mistake.

"Say, Etienne, you know this might sound strange to you . . ."

He looked up from the single bed where he was studying a book by Meyer Baba. His overall appearance was studied neglect, as if he had read all the manuals on human dress and had been unable to incorporate them into his own being. His skin even looked transparent. I finally admitted to myself that Etienne possessed a wisp of immateriality. At any moment, he might dissolve into ether.

"You were about to ask me a question," he chuckled. "Do you still wish to?" His ironic sense of the failure of human efforts gave him his most endearing quality—his sense of humor.

"Well, what I wanted to ask was something I don't think I've ever brought up. I have to ask myself one question all the time: what am I doing this for? Why am I interviewing people about cows that have holes in them? The only suitable answer is that I am being paid to do it. For the life of me, I can't come up with a reason for you.

168

The obvious answer is that you are gathering information for your work at the center, but that's not enough."

"Would it satisfy you to know that for the last few years, right after Mei and I were married and before we came back to Santa Fe to settle down and open the center, we did nothing but conduct interviews like this one today with Angel Gomez."

"My question is why?"

"I have no choice. I must have answers so I can continue to live my life as it must be lived. For eight years I studied Akido. Then I reached a point where it didn't matter if I could deflect a blow coming at my head, or not. It mattered only to know why such a blow had to fall in my direction. So I prepared myself for a different kind of study, and I am not at all disappointed with the results. I am beginning to understand the why of all whys."

"The nature of good and evil?"

"Yes, but more than that. You see, for me all these things are one. To know how to protect yourself is useless. I will tell you why."

I tried to visualize Etienne as an Akido Master.

"Self-defense is after the fact. You are taught to defend yourself only after you have been attacked. So it has taken me some time to discover how to avoid being attacked at all, how to diffuse the emotions that cause violent actions."

"That is what you've been into since you got back from your travels?"

"No, it is what I have been thinking about since I stopped studying Akido in the formal way. This is why the interviews are so important to me. They are showing the way."

"Well, my own answer to that problem is to kick ass wherever and whenever I have to. I was brought up on the law of the wild. When I get scared, I get as crazy as old Gomez."

"Gomez is one type of man who should be regarded as dangerous."

"I don't take him all that seriously."

"You really should."

"I'm not so sure I even take the mutes seriously. In the

beginning they scared the shit out of me—Lorry, too. Then I began to see how unnatural it was. The weirder it gets, the more unbelievable the mute cases, the less I am convinced that any present theory comes close to the truth. No suspect is capable of this sophistication—neither witches nor aliens. I don't know what I'm seeing anymore. Like you told me once, maybe we're all having someone else's bad dream."

"What are some theories that do make sense to you?"

"I spoke with a veterinarian a month ago who claimed to have seen a helicopter landing in back of his house in Cerrillos. Afterward he found a mutilated steer. He saw the copter's lights and runner marks in the sand, and he swore that the steer had been through the same operation Gomez spoke about today: blood collection device, the blown-out guts. The only thing he couldn't explain was the precision cutting of tissue. His opinion was that the whole caper was the work of a bunch of godawful rich Texans who have nothing better to do than spend several million each year mutilating somebody else's cattle."

"That is completely absurd."

"He was a reputable vet in Santa Fe."

"I don't care who he was. He was misled."

"Etienne, I'm not saying he had the answer to what is going on out there, I'm only saying that he had one of the more acceptable answers. I think there are a good ten or more answers we haven't even stumbled into yet, and that's why I'm hacking out these stories one at a time. I want to cover all of most people's ways of thinking: the psychic, scientific, occult, mythical, and maniacal ways that a cow could be taken apart. That's all I'm aiming at."

For the first time he looked at me coldly through narrowed eyes.

"Did I say something wrong?"

"Since you bring it up, I was suddenly thinking of how badly you treated my friend Harjac in that last article. You betrayed his confidence."

I didn't much care what Harjac thought, but I found myself caring what Etienne thought.

"I don't think I did an injustice to Harjac. I think the man is off his rocker, however helpful he may be to some people."

"You should not say such things in print, especially if it hurts someone's feelings."

"Most of what I write is bound to offend somebody for one cockeyed reason or another. I thought that last article was harmless, but I got some hate mail from people who take the UFO business very seriously."

Etienne opened his little satchel and drew out two magazines. "I brought these along just for you. I thought they might help your thinking. Would you mind if I read one of them aloud?"

"Not unless it insults the American way of life."

"Never."

He folded back the cover on *True Space Odysseys*. I had seen magazines like it, but had not bothered to look inside because I considered them trash.

Etienne began to read in his mesmerizing French-American slur:

"On April 19, 1897, at 10:30 P.M., a Kansas farmer named Hamilton, a former member of the House of Representatives, woke to the sound of cattle bawling. Out his window he saw an airship descending upon his cow lot about forty rods from the house. A great turbine wheel, about thirty feet in diameter, which was slowly revolving below the craft, began to buzz and the vessel rose lightly as a bird. Then the craft hovered directly over a two-year-old bawling and kicking heifer, which was caught in the glare of an unearthly light beam and looped about the neck with a cable that swung it up into the air. As the brilliantly lit cigar-shaped airship vanished into the northwest sky, Hamilton began to doubt what he had seen. His bafflement was no less, however, when a neighbor found the butchered hide, head, and legs of Hamilton's heifer in his field."

"Etienne, that stuff's pure fantasy or science fiction; either way, I can't take it seriously. Can you?"

"You take the myths of the American Indians seriously."

"I accept them as myths: as beliefs of the human subconscious.

171

I'll go further than that, to say that beliefs alter behavior. I don't know whether they can actually create a mutilation, but they may have a profound effect on the person who sees one."

"Here are some more mutilation reports that I got from an outfit in Texas. Read them for yourself."

I had seen these before. A self-motivated group of UFO activists sent their findings to anyone who asked. The effort was earnest, anyway. They reported the following:

In Great Sand Dunes, Colorado, September 1967, a full-grown Appaloosa mare was reported stripped of skin in a "surgically precise lifting." Pod marks, scorch marks, and strange odors were found all around the area; the horse's owner, Nellie Lewis, testified that her horse had been mutilated by a UFO.

In Cheyenne Mountain, Colorado (exact date unknown to this writer), a buffalo caged in a zoo was mutilated *within* the confines of its cage. This mutilation took place within close range of a nuclear facility.

In Leadville, Colorado, August 1971, an "Army-colored" helicopter killed forty sheep with a spray of bullets. UPI later reported that an Army investigation revealed that the deaths were the result of a kind of chemical "blistering." No bullet holes were found.

In Crowley and Pueblo Counties, Colorado, September 1975, a policeman fired his 30-30 at an unidentifiable helicopter which made a "whistling sound like air coming out of a fire."

In October 1975 in Cassica County, Idaho, despite the hot sun, meat on the carcass of a mutilated cow appeared fresh and untainted after more than a week of decomposition time.

In the spring of 1976 on a farm near Wildwood, Alberta, Canada, the owner of two healthy horses found both of them dead in a snowbank: each one was missing its uterus and its left eye. Unidentified, nonhuman tracks were located near the scene.

In December 1976 in Logan County, Colorado, a mutilated cow was found in a pasture. Investigators from the sheriff's office reported that the animal was badly decomposed despite sub-zero temperatures.

172

Sometime during the first half of 1977 in Taos County, New Mexico, an insurance claim was paid to a rancher for the mutilation death of a cow whose carcass (in a 24-hour period) changed from reddish brown to grayish white.

"These seem genuine enough," I told Etienne.

His open-hearted grin showed his teeth to their worst advantage. "I am not trying to win you over to my side, as it were. I am only trying to prove to you that there is another side. Harjac is not crazy at all. Something happened to him that he refuses to talk about. I think it was the Galactic affair. Maybe they were not so kind to him as he says. Harjac is only one of the abductees who have come back to earth with stories you would believe if you heard them firsthand."

"I doubt that."

"Is it because you cannot conceive of such a thing as life in outer space? I have a friend named Dr. Daniel Fell who has been aboard an alien spacecraft, and has written a book about it. Someday I will have you meet him. He will change your mind easily."

"There's nothing wrong with my mind the way it is. Listen, you want to know how I feel? I feel that there's got to be life in space. We can shelve that right off the bat. Where I put my foot down is at talk about malign forces and alien interventions in human affairs. Makes no sense to me at all."

"I don't understand it myself, but I believe it is happening. I believe in the negative plane, the inner earth, where forces are combined into a circle of evil influence, as the Indians say. You heard all that from Harjac, and you made fun of it."

"I may have gone too far. The trouble with writing about mutes is that it is very easy to go too far either way. Like Gomez, I say one thing one time, and another another time."

"Have you ever heard the story of Travis Walton?"

"The name's familiar."

"He was probably one of the most famous abductees of all time. He was a logger in the mountains near Heber, Arizona. He and a few friends were talking after work one evening when this thing came out of the sky . . ."

"What kind of thing are we talking about?"

"For lack of a better word, call it a UFO. Anyway, for some reason, Travis Walton ran toward the craft. His friends saw him get trapped in a glowing beam of light which sucked him up into the craft. Walton was missing for six days. He later turned up in a telephone booth in Heber in a confused state of mind. The rest of the story is well-known. Walton was examined by all kinds of doctors, mental and physical, and was subjected to lie detector tests. All reports indicated that the man was telling the truth as he knew it, and so were his friends."

"What was the truth as he knew it?"

"He said, and all this is documented, that he had been captured by creatures that looked like well-developed fetuses. They had completely hairless heads; large brown eyes like an animal's, a lemur's perhaps; and transluscent skin. They examined him and put him back down on earth, unharmed, but of course, shaken by the experience."

"I would be, too."

"So would I, but these stories are now documented by the hundreds. People are coming into the open. Have you read the book called *The Andreasson Affair?*"

"No."

"You should read all these things and then make up your mind who is crazy."

"I promise I will give it more attention, starting tomorrow morning. Right now I am about ready to drift off to sleep."

"Not drift off into space?"

"Who knows?"

"Who knows?" he echoed, switching off the little desk lamp that separated the narrow beds.

That night I didn't close my eyes for a long time. I was obsessed by an old memory. I was about eight years old, and I was climbing Slide Mountain with my bunk mates and my counsellor from

174

summer camp. We had finally made it to the top of the mountain after a knee-scraping climb over rough granite boulders. At the top we made our camp, cooked a bunch of beans in the twilight, and watched the darkness come down from the highest point on any map for five hundred miles. As we sat counting stars, we dozed off.

Everyone was awakened in the early hours of the morning by a bobcat screaming somewhere down the mountain. Alert and just plain scared, we lay in our sleeping bags, told stories, and kept our eyes on the stars, just like before.

The sky didn't lighten, a dense mist shrouded the campsite, and we grew weary of stories and stars and mountains and bobcats. Then it happened: a red burst of intense color zigzagged through the heavens. Every one of us saw it, counsellor included. We were speechless. The bobcat continued to scream in the thick mist, but it was ignored. Someone said, "What is it?" No one answered. The light traced and retraced the same parallelogram pattern. Finally, it dropped right over our heads. We even heard rushing air. Then it was gone. The bobcat quit screaming but none of us slept anymore.

With the hint of dawn, we packed our gear and headed down the mountain. Not until we were safely down on one of the known hiker's trails did any of us want to speak of the night before. In the bright light of day, we got brave and all talked about what we had seen. All of our stories matched, even our counsellor's, who gave what we had seen a name: UFO. He reported our sighting to the nearest Air Force base, and they told him they had gotten other calls on the same sighting. I worked hard to forget the feeling of being dive-bombed by a UFO. Unsuccessfully.

After twenty-odd years, remembering Slide Mountain helped me understand why I was so hard on Harjac, Etienne, and even myself when it came to unknown heights. They scared me. When I was eight, I had learned that such things could and would happen.

I lay in my bed listening to the creek kick against its icy banks. An owl deep in the cottonwoods answered its mate; in deepening winter, owls make love and nestlings happen in hollows in trees and underground. Up here in Dulce the seasons were a month behind

Santa Fe. I lay sleepless listening to the gas burner sputter at the other end of the room. Then I heard the nearby breathing of Etienne. It sounded like there were two Etiennes in the room, one breathing on either side of me, but I knew that was just my overtaxed imagination.

I got way under the covers and dreamed all night about things diving out of the sky on other things: hawks and owls and foul lights and dark mad copters with teeth painted on their hulls and skinless horses frozen under the moon.

22

Angel Gomez was at his gray government office desk when we came in. His filing cabinet was wide open.

"Help yourselves, I got nothing to hide." He waved at us the way he had to Gray Eagle the day before. "Look up anything you want, but put it all back when you're through. Now I'm going to get you cleared," he said picking up the phone. "Then we can go up to Stone Lake and look at that miserable little bull. Yeah, this is Gomez. I want to get clearance from the tribal council for a couple of newspaper guys that want to follow me up to the lake and see that mutilation. Yeah, sure, I'll hold."

"Don't look so worried," he said to me. "They'll let you go. They trust me like a brother. Yeah, I'm still here. It's alright? Okay, you got my word. No, they're good boys. No, they wouldn't do anything like that. They just want to have a look around. Yeah, bye."

Gomez swiveled about in his office chair.

"You're on good behavior today," he announced. "Don't ask a lot of questions. They don't like it if you ask a lot of dumb questions."

"Maybe they think white people are the cause of some of these mutilations," I said.

"If they do, they haven't let on. Burton'll be there again today, you know, the big honcho from the Colorado FBI you saw at San Reymo. He's got jurisdiction all over southern Colorado, but I guess he feels Dulce and points south are his territory as well. Course, after what happened last night, I'm sure he is going to be on the defensive."

"What happened last night?"

"Don't you guys watch the tube? How come I gotta hold your hand and tell you what's going on all the time?" Feet planted on his desk, and one hand propped on the checkered handle of his .38 revolver, he looked like an old-time gunman.

"Funny thing happened last night," he said. "Let's get out to the car and I'll tell you about it." He made room for us on the front seat by throwing a carton of papers in the back.

"This old lady sees a UFO in Taos, then ten minutes later we see the thing up here. Sailed over us at two thousand feet, dropped a beam on a herd of cows. I was four miles away from where it was hovering, and drawing toward it as fast as I could, when one of my men said they were right where it came down."

"What did it look like?" Etienne said.

"That damn thing made no sound at all, and it wasn't even visible until the floodlight beamed down. Then it came real low, moving about ten miles an hour, a round thing with this great light beam coming out of its bottom.

"By the time I hit the cattle guard on the east end of the reservation, the thing was about to take off. When I came around the side road by the gravel plant, I saw red, white, and green lights, the same as an airplane only with more lights.

"It lay there for a second like a big trout trying to figure whether to swim up or down. Then all the lights shut off, it went up, and it

177

headed north-northwest smooth and slow. Didn't move like anything I have ever laid eyes on. No sound, and with all the lights off."

"How come you didn't shoot at it?" said Etienne.

"I didn't have time or I would've gotten off a few shots just to scare it."

"You think you would bring it down that way?"

"Next thing I did was radio Farmington, and Farmington relayed my message to the FAA's air traffic control center in Longmont, Colorado. By God, they picked the thing up on their radar screen traveling at three hundred miles per hour twenty miles north of Albuquerque. Then it just vanished."

We were nearing the open country around Stone Lake. The road came up over a ridge and veered to the right along the north end of the lake. Indian pickups were parked at eighty degree angles to the shore and some families were smoking fish and drinking coffee around small fires. The lake was muddy close to the shore, but further out it was turquoise.

The road veered to the right again and we headed east to a bunch of cars parked under a dark stand of pines. Police and government vehicles were there along with more tribal pickups.

The moment Gomez's car came to a stop, several people came up. A girl with an open note pad was in the lead. I recognized her as a reporter on the *Espanola Sun*. Beside her, wearing a gray raincoat, was Mr. Burton, whom I immediately recognized from San Reymo. Behind these two were a few tribal policemen and a cameraman from the local television station.

Slowly and precisely, Gomez got out of his car, placed his policeman's hat on the dashboard, and picked up his clipboard. He rubbed down his blue-black hair before the cameraman got to him.

A small brown bull was lying on its side. Its hind legs were spread out behind, and its front ones forward, as if it had been running when the mutilation happened. Its expression, unlike others I had seen, was tranquil.

String tied to red stakes marked off an area twenty feet in diameter. The men who stood within the inner sanctum of laboratory string were comparing notes. One said it was an eleven-month-old Charlais-Hereford bull, and that it had all the classic mutilation signs. The incision at its rectum seemed to have been drawn with a compass. The mouth was partly open and newborn flies were milking its glazed eyes. It looked as if it had been born earless and tongueless. Where the back of the mouth opened into the throat passage, a neat v-shaped incision showed where the tongue had been. I kept thinking: *now, here's a case for the SPCA and the den mothers of the world, somebody with a heart ought to see this thing, instead of all these smirking technicians with notebooks and plastic gloves.*

I felt a tap on my shoulder.

"Come on over and meet Mrs. Trujillo," Gomez grinned. "You'll hear a story that tops mine."

A man in a blue winter parka was talking with an old Chicano lady.

"Mrs. Trujillo, I want you to meet a couple of fellows who are up on assignment from *New Mexico Review* in Santa Fe. You don't mind a few more questions, do you?"

"What is it you want to know?" she asked fearfully. "I've told everything I know to these others, and now I want to go home."

"Mrs. Trujillo," Gomez said gently, "we want to hear what happened to you last night just one more time. Then you can go."

He waved over a cameraman and placed himself right next to the woman so the camera focus would include him as well.

"Please go on with what you were saying," he said and grinned toward the whirring lens.

The woman looked apprehensively around her and then, ignoring the cameraman, unexpectedly turned to me and began speaking in a remarkably clear, unaccented voice.

Under a heavy woolen shawl, she was clutching her shoulders to try to get warm. The wrinkles in her leather face spilled inward to meet the dark hollows of her eyes, sunken cheeks, and tight lips.

"I had just gone to bed when the room lit up a bright orange. I thought maybe the neighbors were throwing firecrackers, but it was too bright. I realized it was something else. So I went to the window and opened it, and I could hear crackling. The light was so bright I could see for some distance. At first I thought the neighbor's house was on fire, so I went to the other window.

"Then I saw this form, it was roundish and about as big as two cars, maybe bigger. By then it wasn't orange anymore; it was gray. It stayed for about two minutes. I rushed into another bedroom and opened the drapes. It took off to the north and disappeared in two seconds. All you could see was a red light. It happened so fast. I got real scared; I don't think I went to sleep until five in the morning."

"Wasn't there another sighting of the same craft?" a newsman asked.

"Yes," Gomez confirmed, looking serious and bright at the camera and betraying none of his usual humor. "The same craft we spotted here was seen hovering over a service station near a five hundred-gallon tank truck and a pickup in Taos. Some dust—we don't know yet what it is—was sprinkled on the pickup's cab."

A young man in a brown suit, odd dress for this windy terrain, stepped forward with a microphone. Gomez moved instinctively closer, keeping that confident look.

"You have heard the eye witness account of an actual UFO sighting in Taos," the young man said crisply. "Now let's continue our probe by speaking to Officer Gomez, who has been involved in these mutilation occurrences longer than anyone in the state of New Mexico. Officer Gomez, do you feel the Taos sighting is related to what happened here last night?"

"Right now the lab people think the dust on the pickup has significant levels of potassium and magnesium, the same elements found on the hide of this mutilated bull. It's possible to find them in the soil, but they don't occur naturally in the air."

"So you think that perhaps this dust was sprinkled here and in Taos for some unknown reason?"

"That's right. We think the cattle in this particular area, as well as that truck in Taos, may have been marked for some reason. You see, those elements don't show up except under ultraviolet light. The potassium content on the hides of several of the cattle in this vicinity is seventy times above normal. How it got there, I don't know, and it's not my job to find out. That's up to Schoenfeld Laboratories at the moment."

"Officer Gomez, you've seen plenty of strange things up here in Apache land. What do you think of Mrs. Trujillo's story?"

"I have no comment, but I am curious about the yellow-colored, petroleum-based substance we found by this mutilated bull."

"What are the findings on that, Officer Gomez?"

"The results of that test aren't in yet, but I'd say that petroleum is like nothing we know about at the present time."

"How do we know that it's a petroleum?"

"We don't. This game has plenty of questions and no answers—like the liver of this little bull. When we found it lying by the carcass, it was all white and mushy. Now the lab men say there are calcium, magnesium, and phosphorus in it. There are also some unidentified burns on this animal's hind legs where the rectum was removed."

"Are these laser burns?"

"I have no idea. They have acid in them, but the fur wasn't singed or burned by anything heated. All I can say for sure is whoever's responsible for this mutilation has more money than our government's got."

"I know of no sophisticated muffling equipment that could hush the rotors on a helicopter," Burton was saying to a reporter from the *Rio Grande Sun*.

"What do you think of the remark that the sighting was a classified government machine?"

"I don't know where you guys get that stuff. Not a helicopter in existence can fly three hundred miles an hour. Nothing at the Kirtland Air Force Base fits the bill. What's more, the thing lifted over twelve- to thirteen-thousand-foot peaks."

"Can you explain," a man in jeans and a cowboy hat said, "why there was no log report at the FAA, even though Officer Gomez says his message was called in last night."

"I have no comment on that except that it is not common to log all the flights that come in."

"Are you presently using psychics to interpret certain data?" a woman asked.

"No comment."

"Our paper would like to know what your agency thinks of this picture." A man in a tailored suit held up a four by five inch print of the mutilated body of a cow. A pillar of white mist was coming out of the incisions in the animal's stomach. The man holding the photograph had a *New York Times* identification tag.

"I am told," Burton said cautiously, "that these rather bizarre images turn up only in the developing tray. They are picked up by infrared film, not seen by the human eye. I have no idea what they represent, but to us they're unscientific."

"We want to know what they are," someone shouted.

"So do I," said Burton.

A woman in her early thirties wearing a ski parka pushed her way to the center of the group. "Senator Salisbury is pressing for a major FBI investigation. We'd like to know exactly what efforts your agency has made, Mr. Burton, to track down mutilations in our state of Colorado."

Burton looked resentful. "You really have it in for us, don't you? It doesn't matter if we're doing our job to the best of our ability as long as you've got a scapegoat."

"Can you tell the difference between pork and beef?" a familiar voice called out. When I turned to see who had spoken, Officer Gomez was staring at his polished trooper's boots, his arms crossed casually.

"The majority of our efforts have produced no definite results," Burton said, ignoring the comment, "but we've maintained daily checks on flight schedules at Fort Carson, we've kept in close touch with the Department of the Interior, we've worked with wildlife research teams and undercover investigative teams—all in the hope of pulling something tangible out of nothing.

"Our findings in over twenty-three recent mutilation cases demonstrated that only nineteen postmortems were good enough to yield a reasonable pathological exam. Roughly ten of those nineteen died a natural death: five were killed by predators and five died of unknown causes. Only four were willfully mutilated by a sharp instrument, which could have been predator-related. In other words, claws or fangs. So, we don't know, do we?"

"When will you know?" I asked.

Burton leveled his cold gray eyes at me. He was not going to tell the press anything he didn't want them to know. Unlike the last time I had seen him at San Reymo, he was no longer an investigator, he was a spokesman. *Word* had come down.

"As an investigator of mutilations in Colorado," he continued like a tape recorder, "I've been unable to determine for a fact that a person was involved in the more than two hundred cases which were examined. Does that answer your question, young man? The bottom line is to go about your work in a sensible manner. If you want quicker results than I've been able to get, all I can say is good luck, because you've got a tremendous job on your hands."

He pushed his way to his car, threw his great bulk into the driver's side, and slammed the door.

"There's the kind of man that made this country what it is today—a mess." Gomez was the town marshal being confronted by the big-money political wheeler-dealer just off the train. "You know what he told me, that sonofabitch," he spat. "He said that that colt they found up in Arapaho County was mutilated by juveniles. He told me that out of twenty mutilations in Wyoming, nineteen were classified death from natural causes. He even went so far as to say that predators were responsible for all the recent mutilations in Oregon, Idaho, and Nebraska, every one of them. If that thing I saw last night was a predator, there ought to be one hell of a good bounty on it."

We walked back to Gomez' car. In Etienne's eyes was a bemused look.

"What did you find out?" I asked.

"Everything and nothing."

As we drove off, the two, gloved men were putting the young bull into a green bag. I wondered what unidentified silver particles remained in the tunnels of its inner ears.

23

Etienne had arranged for us to interview Dr. Daniel Fell, who claimed that while working as technical engineer at the White Sands Proving Grounds he had observed and then ridden in a flying saucer. A sworn recluse, he had never allowed his comments on ufology and its relationship to mutes to appear in any major newspaper.

Our destination for nightfall was Sierra Blanca. On this mountain a few days earlier, two fighter planes had last been tracked by radar before they vanished into thin air. It was just one of many recent incidents that the Air Force played down as "lost aircraft, nothing too surprising." The higher altitude of the mountain would be ideal for observing the sky for UFOs, about which Etienne was a fanatic. I didn't mind as long as it was on the way.

Military officials said the two planes had been on an air combat training mission out of Holloman Air Force Base near Alamogordo. They had been modified to resemble Soviet MIG fighters, one camouflaged and the other silver, both bearing red stars on the tail.

A thorough ground search covered the deep canyon and heavy underbrush foothills southeast of Carrizozo for the F–5 jets and their missing pilots. At least twenty civilian aircraft flew twelve hours daily for eleven days, and Army aircraft from the National Range Operations Directorate racked up 122 search hours. The recovery mission had been suspended.

The expression "vanished into thin air" is especially apt in New Mexico, where the deep cobalt or turquoise sky has compelled poetic delirium. Tricks of light and air are common in the desert. As we neared Carrizozo at dusk, dark clouds appeared from nowhere and capped the heavens. The sun glinted at the horizon, creating a cave world illumined by an underground sun.

The sun flamed pink and we were inside a circus tent. Each green *cholla* threw a razor-blue shadow, each bunch of sagebrush glowed on the red earth.

"You know," I said to Etienne, "it's hard to believe that anything could get lost in this bright, clean place. Then, there is so much of it to get lost in."

"Time is the key to missing planes as well as missing persons," he replied. "Those fighter planes may have just taken off now. In another time frame, they have not left the ground. To say they have disappeared does not explain a thing. It's a convenience."

"What do you mean by a convenience?"

"Well, it is quite common, even in the cattle mutilations, for something lost to turn up again as in the case of Travis Walton or the missing calf that just appeared a month after its disappearance. This makes me wonder whether they are ever lost in the first place, or whether we are using terms that conveniently explain our not seeing them."

"You think the Air Force coverups are also for convenience?"

"Certainly. Did you ever hear of the Lubbock Lights?"

"They were in *Project Blue Book*, if I remember right."

"They were described by observers as soft blue lights forming a flying wing one and a half times the size of a B–36. An employee of the Atomic Energy Commission at Sandia got a good look. This was in 1951. Just twenty minutes after the Albuquerque sighting, four professors from Texas Tech in Lubbock saw the same lights pass overhead. The incident is kept quiet, but it isn't hushed up as cleverly as the Socorro sighting in 1964."

"That was the one where a policeman, a guy like Angel Gomez, saw a spacecraft land in the desert. He claimed two humanoids got out and that they wore white coveralls."

"The significant thing was the official report. The Air Force and FBI agents assigned to the Socorro coverup told the policeman not to mention the pyramid symbol that he saw on the side of the craft, and especially not to mention the two small figures."

"I seem to remember a lab analysis of a rock found near the landing that had foreign matter on it."

"That was a zinc and iron alloy in a combination of elements unavailable to us."

"But all this was quite common in the fifties," I said. "Remember Farmington? The town was bombarded by UFOs in March of 1950. Massive daylight flights of silver discs caused all hell to break out for days on end in that town. Half the population of Farmington reported seeing them. The media played it for all it was worth, but no one, outside of the actual observers, gave it the least credibility."

"I guess it's not so surprising," Etienne said, "that the cattle investigations have taken over eleven years to get officially off the ground."

We drove up Sierra Blanca in the dark. We pitched a two-man pup tent off the road below the snow line and ate a couple of sandwiches in the dark. Moths dive-bombed us and pelted the tent once we were inside.

Once in my bag, I dropped off into a deep sleep that was unbroken until dawn when my eyes popped open. I had an aftertaste of a strange dream. In the dream, I was lying in the tent when strange hands began to brush the canvas. Whether they belonged to lost fighter pilots, extraterrestrials or a curious bear, I could not have said, but the sensation of exploratory hands or paws went far into my unconscious. Then the dream changed and my own hands were in the mouth of something, being licked. A slight pressure was applied to them. It did not hurt, but I wanted to cry out.

The next morning, Etienne listened to my story with an attentive, detached expression.

186

"We were approached last night," he said flatly.

"What do you mean—approached?"

"It was definitely outside the tent. I didn't fall asleep until it went away about four."

"Did you hear animal feet on the ground? Were there sounds of movement, or intrusion, or what?"

"Before it left, I heard it breathing."

"Jesus. You heard something—a bear most likely—inches from our heads, and you didn't wake me up."

"I was concerned that I would scare it into doing something it wouldn't normally have done."

"Are we talking about a coyote, a bear, or what? How big was this thing?"

"I do not think it meant to harm us. Whatever it was, it went away peacefully. It wasn't a bear, definitely not. What I heard sounded like an old, tired man trying to get his breath back."

"Outside our tent at ten thousand feet up Sierra Blanca?"

"Yes."

"I'd rather think it was a starved grizzly than a weird old man in the middle of the night in the middle of nowhere."

"If I hear anything tomorrow night, I will wake you."

"Thanks for the reassurance."

As we drove away from the campsite, the silence was strained. It unnerved me to think that Etienne had been lying there next to me, listening to some peculiar noise—which probably had a logical explanation—without bothering to wake me up.

After a big breakfast in the town of Ruidoso we both felt more like ourselves. We even made jokes about a Sierra Blanca ghost who wanted to pass the time with us before the hour of sunrise, but the joke didn't stay with me. What did was the sensation of having my hands in the mouth of something I could not identify.

24

Coming down from the ponderosa meadows of Ruidoso and the lower desert, we saw far away the long white scar trembling in the sun: White Sands. The next town down from Ruidoso was Tularosa, a patch of green with irrigation smells and small secure lawns. At ten o'clock we arrived in Alamogordo, a town made possible by Air Force personnel.

Dr. Daniel Fell lived at the west end of town in a common gray tract house. A tired but bright-eyed man in his mid-sixties, he took us into the living room, where his wife offered coffee and some comfortable chairs.

In his careworn face were hounded eyes, and his speech was punctuated with short breaths.

Etienne explained that we were interviewing people who had clues to the cattle mutilations. We had chosen him, he said, because of his well-publicized experience in a saucer. In his opinion, were the two events—saucers and mutilations—related?

"I will tell you something," he snapped, "and you may or may not believe me. I have not bothered to follow the cattle mutilations in the papers or anywhere else. It's perfectly obvious that extraterrestrials, as they're being called nowadays, have as much interest in us as we have in them."

Dr. Fell's wife, a thin white-haired woman with a face that seemed on the verge of tears, entered the room and admonished, "Don't you think *they* have as much right to look at us as we do them? Our friends in space are medical technicians as well as scientists, travelers, and what have you. Sugar or cream? Let me warm your cup for you."

"Dr. Fell," Etienne asked, "what do you think of etheric beings? Since no one ever sees the mutilating, do you think there's a possibility that some are being done by beings that we could not see even if we wanted to?"

Dr. Fell brought the fingertips of both hands together. He looked like he was preparing to execute a magic trick.

"When I was on lecture circuits, I used to answer that question by flashing a silver dollar. I'd say, 'To you, this looks pretty solid, but to a scientist, it isn't. That's because only one million-millionth part of the average atom is occupied by nuclear particles. The rest is occupied by space.'

"I was getting at the fact that almost any nuclear arrangement other than what we perceive as normal could seem awfully improbable. Yes, I believe in etheric beings, but I also believe in beings made of lead, to whom we earthlings must seem so etheric as to be invisible."

"What is the possibility," I asked, "that some mutilations are the work of beings that are, in some sense, malign? I know that sounds a trifle Hollywood, but—"

Dr. Frey screwed up his face. "Listen, son, good and evil are the most relative terms we have. We define good as what is good for us. Don't you think there are those up there who would differ with us? It could be very good for them to remove the heart of a cow and carry it a million miles away."

"Would you agree that we may have enemies in outer space?"

"An enemy is someone or something who wants something you have. Conversely, an enemy can be someone or something who has something you want. Does that answer the question?"

"If they are more advanced than we are, what could they possibly want that we have?" Etienne asked.

"Maybe they want nothing more than a legal landing field. Did you know that it's impossible to legally visit earth from space? You couldn't legally answer an alien's radio message, because you would be communicating with an unlicensed vehicle. Extraterrestrials are the ultimate illegal aliens. Without a birth certificate, a health certificate, and God knows what else, they couldn't save us from our own inherent self-destruction, even if they wanted to."

"Would you mind telling us what happened the night of July 4?"

"You sound like an attorney," he bristled. "Why don't you read my book for that information? That's why I wrote it."

"I have read your book, but there is one thing I don't understand: why didn't you run away when the craft approached? It would have been a normal reaction."

"If there's one thing Dr. Fell isn't, it's normal," his wife said. "It should be obvious to you young fellows by now that this is no average mind. Dr. Fell is one of the most brilliant intelligences we have today, and that was why he was chosen."

"That's alright, dear. I can come to my own defense, if I need to. Well, to answer your question, I have to ask one of my own. Why did a group of my men leave the proving grounds to witness a fireworks display in Las Cruces? Here were men who spent every day of their lives playing around with rocket nozzles. You'd think they would have been sick of rocketry. Well, in fact, they weren't. Watching a fireworks display was a free ride for them, just like a sailor rowing a boat in a public park when he's on shore leave. Those men could watch rockets explode all night and not worry about whether anybody was going to get hurt.

"Aerojet, the company I worked for, provided a limousine to take us into town, but there wasn't room in the car for me without crowding, so I offered to take the bus. The dispatcher told me that the bus for Las Cruces would depart at 7:30, so I went back to my room to read a book. At about 7:30, I showed up at the motor pool and discovered that the dispatcher had been dead wrong about the departure time, and the bus had already left.

"So I was stuck at White Sands on one of the hottest nights of the year. I went back to my room. Those wooden barracks were burning hot, but with the air conditioning, it was bearable and I settled back down to read my book. Then the air conditioning quit. I knew I couldn't fix it because it was up on the roof. It was cooler outdoors, so I decided to take a little walk out in the desert.

"I was walking toward our test stand about a mile from the base when I spotted a dirt road. I'd never been on it before, so I took it.

190

"It was nine o'clock—the sun was down but the sky was still fairly light—when I saw a star blink out, then another to the right of it, and two more below it. Twenty or so seconds passed, and I saw that the original star did not come into view. Then I saw something descending at an angle of about forty-five degrees. I described it later as an oblate spheroid, but at the time, the only thought that registered with me was that its bearing was constant.

"It came within twenty feet of where I was standing, touched the ground at zero velocity, and settled on a clump of stout brush. The thing was twenty feet in diameter and about sixteen feet high."

"Didn't you want to run from it?" asked Etienne.

"I have been asked that question thousands of times. Of course, I was scared, but like a cat that has the forethought not to run before the approach of a dog, I decided to stay put. An even greater deterrent—this puzzled me until it was explained to me later—was the vision I kept having of all the men back at the base laughing at me."

"What did the surface of the object look like?"

"Silver. It didn't have the hard, bright finish of nickel or chromium. It most resembled platinum, impervious to corrosion. Naturally, my next impulse was to touch it with my hand, curiosity being as strong an impulse as fear.

"At that point my scientific mind was at work. I was pondering: if the craft had approached earth from the sunlit side of the planet, its surface ought to be warm. On the other hand, if it had come from the shadow side, it would have been cool. When I stepped up and touched it, the surface was totally frictionless, as if ten thousand infinitesimal ball bearings were between my fingers and the metal. The oil on your skin will provide drag on even the smoothest of glass, so this was unbelievable. Then a sharp voice crackled: 'Better not touch the hull, pal, it's still hot.' "

"When I read that in your book, I was surprised. Forgive me, but it doesn't sound real," I said.

"Of course, it's as fake as a four dollar bill. It was explained to me later, too."

"What happened next?"

"The rest of the story has been told and retold and is quite boring to me now. I took a ride in that saucer to New York City and back in one-half hour. The inside of the craft was bare, almost ascetic, and there was no pilot. Later on, I learned that it was remote-controlled. The voice I was hearing was beaming down from the mother ship somewhere off in space."

"The voice, then, was a telepathic communication?"

"For lack of a better word. Actually, the pilot spoke to me through a direct modulation of the auditory nerve. The effect on the brain was the same, but there were no sound waves."

"Was it also possible that the pilot had been tampering with your thoughts prior to the flight?" Etienne asked.

"I don't consider psychic contact of extraterrestrials to be tampering. How else are they to communicate with us? This is their only legal means. If you want to get technical about it: there is a pact within the Galactic Confederation which forbids outright mind control. It is like a Monroe Doctrine of the universe."

Dr. Fell sipped his coffee. It had grown cold, but he did not seem to notice. He seemed to be living outside of his physical body. Perhaps that was why at first I had thought him insensitive.

"I was also to learn from the pilot of that little remote-controlled craft—his name was Al-lan—that he had broken this pact in order to set me up for the flight. He had arranged things to his advantage.

"For instance, when I was considering running away when I first saw the thing, Al-lan made me see what would have happened: the derision of my staff. Oh, there'd been many UFO sightings at White Sands, but none of them on this order. So he prevented me from making a fool of myself, while keeping me there so I could ride in the saucer. He also arranged for the dispatcher to say 7:30 instead of 7:00."

"Was the breakdown of the air conditioning also prearranged?" I asked.

"Well, that happened all the time, but he did make me want to take a walk on that deserted road. I felt quite a compulsion to walk on it by myself, even though it was still hot outside."

192

"You don't consider any of this to be tampering with your mind?" said Etienne.

"Not after I learned what Al-lan was trying to accomplish on this planet," he said dramatically. "Al-lan explained to me on that first flight, and on subsequent contacts, that he was an emissary ordered to ensure the continuance of this planet. After the discovery of the atomic bomb, many extraterrestrials doubted we'd go the distance. When people ask me if Al-lan's mission was successful, I always refer them to the obvious: we're still here."

"Did you ever actually meet Al-lan?"

"Was I ever in his physical presence? Yes. I once flew on TWA with him from Medford, Oregon, to Sacramento, California. After the White Sands incident, Al-lan enlisted my assistance in various ways. I provided him with a bank account, birth certificate, immunization papers, and other necessary things. He scolded me for not making his message clear to all earth people—but I'm getting ahead of myself. At first, he wanted secrecy. His greatest test, this being with powers far beyond our grasp, was to look so average in every way that you'd walk by him on the street and not know."

"How long did this naturalization process take?" I asked.

"About four of our earth years, I would guess. Then he spent around three weeks with me up in Oregon. That was the second visit."

"I don't believe you have mentioned that one."

"Well, four years had passed from the time I rode to New York and back in the little craft. I hadn't told a soul about it, hadn't even thought of writing my book. I was up near Medford, Oregon, where we have a small cabin on eighty acres. You get to it by a three-mile deserted road. It's an isolated place, but that's why we like it. Anyway, I'd gone into town to get some supplies. Coming back on that three-mile road, I rounded a turn and there it was, a small saucer like the one I'd ridden in. It was dusk. There, standing by the barn, was a man I'd never seen before. He was just standing there, a stranger, dressed like any one of us."

"Al-lan."

"Yes, I knew it the moment I laid eyes on him. The rest is almost comic. I taught him how to drive, which was damned hard for him to do, because whenever he came to a stop sign or cross traffic, I had to demand that he stop. His inclination was to increase acceleration and go right over any obstacle in his path. The notion of braking seemed absurd to him."

"So you spent three weeks training him to be an earth person?"

"I mostly fine-tuned things he'd already studied, tidied up his grammar, that sort of thing. My main contributions were teaching him how to drive and finding him a job."

"Where did he work?"

"He became, in almost no time at all, a successful import and export entrepreneur. That position afforded him time to troubleshoot for the betterment of mankind. He was based in the Middle East, Egypt, and Israel."

"Do you think he was successful in his efforts to help us?" I asked.

"If he hadn't been—and this is what I keep telling people—we'd be an incandescent gas floating around the atmosphere."

"I assume that Al-lan's powers of thought transference were used for our benefit," Etienne said.

"That is entirely correct."

"What were his methods?"

"He simply put a picture in someone's brain. This picture would stay there until that person let go of all his destructive mental energies."

"What was the picture, specifically?"

"He made one of our world leaders hear the wail of two billion people burning. Needless to say, Al-lan prevented a Third World War, a number of times."

"Is he still with us?" I asked.

"Al-lan was tragically disappointed with his work. He did not accomplish what he set out to do. He once told me that earth people were children unwilling to accept manhood."

"That isn't to say he has gone from our lives," said Mrs. Fell. "He happens to be with us right now."

"But not in the physical sense," he corrected. "He has gone from us in that way."

"Al-lan is not gone as long as you are here," she replied.

He looked out into the furnace of sunlight like a man caught in a body no longer alive.

"Hot out there," he said. "Hotter'n blazes."

White Sands: two hundred and thirty square miles of gypsum sand. Standing in the white immensity of concave shapes, you feel like the lone survivor of a dead star.

Etienne and I, after leaving the home of Dr. Fell, drove on to White Sands and wandered around for almost four hours. Then we sat on a high white crest, listening to the dry buzz of wind in the moving crystals. Before our eyes were mile upon mile of skunk bush, yucca, rabbit brush, saltbush, and cottonwood.

I wondered, sitting there with the wind in my ears, how many Al-lans had set up camp in the womanly curves of the dunes. I saw the pink stains on the carcasses of mutilated cattle; and the Carrizozo plains gone in a pink cloud at sunset; the pink of the Sangre de Cristos, Blood of Christ Mountains; and Christ's imitators, the Penitentes, cactus-whipped and bleeding.

The shape of a dune and the shape of a saucer are similar. The little sickle dunes, called *barchans*, look exactly the same. When the wind blows, it moves the sand along the edges of the sickle dune faster than the sand in the center, which shapes the sickle more pointedly and drives it along in lines sixty miles long. *Barchans* can maneuver over anything, including high plateaus.

I thought of the *barchan*-like crafts seen over the Tularosa Basin, as Dr. Fell had said, moving as light upon the air, as natural as the soundless, frictionless sprawl of *barchans*.

The endless fascination with light and dark: on one side of the Sands lives a white mouse, and where the white gypsum ends and the

195

crystals are black, there's a black mouse. If the black one ever strays to the white sand, it is plucked by a hawk. This plucking is the natural order. In the opinion of the mouse, if such there be, the hawk is evil; but in the mind of the hawk, the mouse, its heart beating in the air, is merely there to be taken.

25

At dusk, we drove deep into the Mescalero Reservation to a place, high in the pines, that Etienne identified as "just like the spot where Travis Walton was taken." A forestry crew had recently logged the area, and their leavings were everywhere, so we made a fine pine-bough bed to go under our pup tent.

The last light lay in the basin at ten o'clock, and we could still see the surface of White Sands more than sixty miles down in the desert. We rested on the hood of the car and sipped black coffee. The stars spilled all the way into the ponderosas and firs. The wind was no longer the warm savory breeze of the desert, but a high mountain wind with cutting edge.

"I have had the feeling, since I was a child," Etienne said coolly, "that I would one day be taken."

"I wonder how Mei and your little girl would react to such a thought. Have you ever told them?"

"The little girl, no. Mei, yes. She has accepted it. Once, when I was a boy living in France, my best friend had a disturbing dream and he looked out his window. Down in the cow pasture was a flying saucer. At one of the openings at its side, he was astonished to see me

196

waving at him. Ever since then I have been in touch with contactees all over the world. I know as surely as I sit here with you, looking up at the stars, that one day I will be taken."

"There are too many negative associations in my mind with the word taken."

"It scares me, too. I would not want to be taken in that way, but that is not the message I send. Why should harm come to me? Look quickly, there it goes. Did you see it?"

A blue star wiggled across the sky.

"Maybe we will be taken together," Etienne chuckled.

"I'm not that disposed to go."

"Then probably they will not take you. Let me tell you something: I have this ability to see something in the sky just before anyone else. I don't know why, but it is true. I can also sense danger, as you know."

I was staring into the sky in the perverse hope of spotting a moving light in advance of Etienne. As if on command, a light was moving steadily.

"Etienne, to the left of those pines, a slow steady arc, like a falling star in slow motion."

"A satellite," he said dryly, "but they are all satellites until they are something else."

Before going into the tent for the night, he spotted two more lights, one so pastel and soft that I had to close one eye to see it at all. Once inside the tent, we were zipped in an empty belly of darkness. The only light was the face of my watch.

It was eleven o'clock, the wind growling around the tent, when we drifted off to sleep. It was 3:26 when I suddenly awoke. I heard Etienne breathing inside the tent, and the same deep breathing on the other side of the canvas, inches from my right ear: intermittent, yet unison breathings. The sound outside was definitely not an animal; it didn't have the depth or penetration of a bear or an elk, or even a coyote. It was Etienne's breath.

I put my index finger over my right ear and shut out the outside breathing. The inside breathing continued its steady pulse. I reversed fingers and ears. When I released my ears and listened naturally, both breathings were again present.

Fear gave way to the attraction of mystery. Convinced that I was not imagining things, I lay back and listened. Half the night passed and I lay immobile. Etienne never awoke or moved, and the eerie repetitions stayed on course. I decided that if I were mad for hearing two Etiennes, then I had to accept it as calmly as he would accept his passage to a distant star.

First light finally came, and Etienne woke up. I told him what had happened. He looked like a thief caught in the act.

"What you experienced was only natural."

He said that one night when his wife had moved to the foldaway bed in their living room because he had been kicking her in his sleep, she awoke to see Etienne standing off the floor. She could hear him breathing in the bedroom, and he was also standing and breathing in the living room. A voice told her not to worry, but she was naturally very frightened and got out of bed to embrace him. The body she embraced was made of air, but the body of Etienne in the bedroom was real and sound asleep.

"It is not so hard to do. You can do it."

"What about the other night. Was that you awake hearing yourself asleep?"

"No. I think that was Dr. Fell warning us about something."

Sunday night, after the three-hundred-mile drive back to Santa Fe, a thought came into my mind. I propped a pillow under my head and settled in with a good book, but the thought did not go away.

Monday morning, as I shaved for work, the thought was still there. It did not come and go as thoughts do that haunt, nag, or bother. Other thoughts went by it and did not distract it.

At the office, clippings and telephone calls reported this or that event. There was news of Len Kreuger's mute investigation. He was going to get to the bottom of things, the papers said, but he was not saying anything to anyone, least of all the media. That solid German name and face committed to justice seemed to give him undeserved credibility. There were clippings about his effective presence on local radio and TV, but his assertions added up to nothing.

"Well, dear," Marsha said leaning against the doorjamb of my office, "you may now go on to bigger and better things. Looks like Mr. Kreuger has it all figured out. Oh, there's that phone again."

It was one of those mornings when dread wells up for no apparent reason. A band of tension tightens around the base of the skull, not an incipient headache but an apprehension.

Marsha came back. She wore a gold amulet on a pretty gold chain around her neck, and the blue morning light from the window in the office opposite turned her dark blue dress to gauze. She stood looking at me inquisitively. She seemed so reassuring and casual that I wanted to share with her the thought that had come in the back door of my mind the day before, but I reasoned that voicing it might dignify its existence. Etienne had warned me of this. Suddenly I was suspicious of everyone. I wanted to heave my portable Adler out the window. Instead I asked Marsha a question.

"Have you ever had a thought that wouldn't leave you alone?"

"A menacing one?"

"An image of something you don't want to see."

"Once I saw a baby dying before it was born. It happened in my mind before it really happened."

"Your baby or someone else's?"

"Someone else's. Someone I was close to."

"You were probably reading your friend's mind. You psychically emphathized with her trauma."

"I never bothered to figure it out. It happened, that's all. There's the phone."

I heard her feet move down the hall to the switchboard, then the feet of others, Jamie's among them.

"Did you hear the one about tuna fish?" a voice said.

"That was absolutely gross, Thomas." Jamie had pronounced his disdain for Thomas's obvious lack of refinement.

I felt his instant admonishment as he passed the open doorway. "Well, hello, big boy. What are you staring at the ceiling for?" The smile on his smooth, youthful face cast gloom into my own grim world of the moment. "You had better not sit with glass eyes this morning. Not after last night's announcement on the six o'clock news."

"I've already read about it. He doesn't know a thing."

"Well, how could an FBI novice who has only been a professional snoop for twenty-five years have a nickel's worth of insight anyway?"

"Don't harp on me this morning. I drove three hundred miles yesterday and I'm road weary."

"Well, I'm glad to hear you're performing your duties. Go out and interview Kreuger."

He vanished and Thomas took his place.

"Tell a guy a joke and he holds it against you," Thomas mumbled.

I yawned, my head beginning to hurt.

"Am I keeping you up?" Thomas asked.

All at once a spring popped loose in my head. I got to my feet, walked to the shipping room, and out the loading entrance. Then I was out the door walking freely in the sun toward the plaza.

Almost immediately, the pressure was off. I sat on an empty park bench and looked toward the Palace of the Governors. The Indians were laying down their black bowls and silver jewelry. The sun topping the high branches of the cottonwoods and the slow movements of the women setting up their blankets were helping me.

Then I realized that I had been most disturbed by the sound the thought had made. The thought was leaving, and now it seemed safe to think about it.

I thought I knew where it had come from, but I was afraid to admit it. It had started when I was leaving the reservation. I remembered seeing the gleaming hills after the ascent from the stony desert above Tularosa.

I was looking at a band of Indian ponies and thinking that nothing on earth has the precise grace of a long-legged Appaloosa horse dancing on a dark green hill. I was staring at a horse, when I suddenly saw it standing frozen in the moon, its flesh surgically shorn from its head and shoulders and back. I heard the sound of living flesh being peeled back and ripped from the pink-muscled perfection of that animal. The eyes of the horse were wild with fear.

Etienne had once told me, early in our relationship, "You must be watchful of your thoughts. Keep yourself pure. If you fail at this, you will invite dangerous thoughts to inhabit you."

At the time, my reaction to his warning had been casual. I knew it was psychologically possible to invite bad thoughts by opening yourself to them, but a mind jam has to be experienced to be believed.

For eighteen hours, the thought had lived in me like a parasite. At irregular intervals, I'd become its helpless captive. I'd see in my mind the dappled skin torn from the muscled sinews of an Appaloosa mare.

I wanted to explain it away by saying: Yes, like everyone else involved in mutilation investigations, I was preyed upon by an image from one of the most famous mute cases: an Appaloosa standing dead in the starlight and a girl crying helplessly when she found it in the morning.

Logic failed when I considered Al-lan's mind-bending powers, which had helped Dr. Fell arrive at the appointed place in the desert. Thoughts that supported a necessary cause were, according to Al-lan, permissible. Had I fallen unsuspectingly into a mind trap—negative, positive, or both?

Had it been initiated by Dr. Fell himself? Thinking back, the man's droning voice had been both reassuring and troubling, like the contrast of his uncommon thoughts to his banal suburban home. His manner of breathing came back to me: each word was punctuated with gasps for air.

I returned to both nights in the tent, the dream of the thing that held my hands in its mouth and the two breathings that I supposed were Etienne. Had they been Dr. Fell all along, or was I completely out of my mind?

True, in recent weeks, I had found myself becoming obsessed

with mutilation cases, but that was plain old fatigue, not mind control. If I was suffering, was it for a reason? There were too many unanswerable questions.

That night at home, I told my wife I wanted to quit the *Review*. She didn't argue.

26

Jamie sat as composed as a Buddhist businessman when I gave him my resignation. Smiling, he handed me a check.

"This is for leave time. I could see it coming from a long way away."

My hand reached for the check, but I was reluctant to take it, especially since I had prepared such a sweet little going away speech.

"Let me tell you a story about a friend of mine," Jamie said. "Maybe you've heard me mention the name Pamela Gibbs? She has a big black cat that likes to hunt. Not long ago, this cat brought home a fat horned toad and dropped it in her bathtub. Pamela had never seen one close at hand, so she studied it carefully. The cat studied her at the same time, and then something clicked in that cat's brain. It disappeared, and when it returned, there was another horned toad in the tub. Then another and another until Pamela was up to her ears in horned toads."

"I'm afraid I don't get the connection."

"That's because it's so plain." He picked up a sheaf of papers from his desk. I recognized the double-spaced reports with inked corrections in my own handwriting.

"What we have here is a pile of horned toads. Now, what you

need to do is go off somewhere—like Pamela Gibbs' cat did, because she told it to—and take a rest in the shade. If an ugly old horned toad rears its head, you look the other way. I'll expect to see you the beginning of next week; meanwhile we're going to run the first in a series of your reports. I think we may win one of those awards over there." He nodded at a plaque from the New Mexico Press Association, a prize for reportorial excellence awarded to the *Review* the year before.

As I walked out the door, he was typing ninety to a hundred words a minute, that smile back on his lips.

A week in the woods, that was what I needed. Then, if I was back harvesting horned toads, it would be different. I would know how to bag them better, anyway—with gloves.

At home, I mixed a shandy—half beer, half lemonade—and packed a rucksack with enough clothes to last a week. I knew a plan would come once I slipped on my worn-soled Dunham boots. There were plenty of possibilities: Lake Catherine on the other side of the ski basin; Horse Thief Canyon, deep in the Pecos; or even the Hot Springs at Jemez.

I packed absentmindedly in the upstairs bedroom, looking out the concave adobe window at the morning light on the piñons. A warm wind was moving their branches ever so slightly, and I knew the camping would be good. Just getting away would be good.

Lorry came up in the Jeep truck owned by my cousin, Peter, who was living with us at the time. Brown supermarket bags were lined up in its bed. The truck stopped, the engine shuddered, and the wheels lurched forward in the dust as she put it in gear and let off the clutch.

Suddenly I broke into a cold sweat. Lorry was outside the truck with two grocery bags in her arms. She was stepping in front of the left headlight when I yelled, "Don't." My voice was at full volume and it scared me as much as it did her. She hesitated and glanced at the upstairs window.

"What's the matter?" she shouted with an irritated look. "You scared me half to death."

"Is the truck okay?" I asked feebly.

"Of course it is. What's the matter with you?"

"I gotta get out of here. I'm going berserk. Sorry if I shouted."

She held her position by the left front headlight.

"Can I walk inside now?" she asked sarcastically.

I felt incredibly stupid.

Then the truck's engine suddenly charged up, the back tires churned in the sand, and the truck leaped headlong down the incline that ended with the house. Before she could jump to one side, Lorry was struck on the arm that clutched the bag of groceries. She fell backwards away from the truck. The riderless Jeep crashed into a wheelbarrow under the kitchen window. The wheelbarrow hooked itself neatly to the front differential and brought the truck to a crunching halt.

Lorry was sobbing in the dust, her hands covering her face. Groceries were strewn everywhere. She had a bunch of celery in her right hand, all that was left of the bag. The Jeep's left headlight had hit it head on.

"Celery's good medicine," I said.

"Celery saved my life."

We hugged each other and both of us began to laugh and cry at the same time. We were still hugging each other when Peter drove up the driveway and saw the mess of groceries and the Jeep that had swallowed a wheelbarrow.

Peter has the deliberate ease of a Danish shipbuilder. The fact that he'd loaned us his truck and that now it was a destructo-machine, and that it was unmercifully intertwined with a wheelbarrow didn't unnerve him. He poked under the hood as we gathered up crushed cans of Campbell's soup.

"What happened," he said, "is that the starter wire got loose, touched against something hot, and caused a short in the electrical system, which itself caused the engine to turn over at least once before it died. By then the pistons had jumped, the wheels had turned, and since you were parked on a hill—well, it kind of took off, didn't it?"

"The engine started like someone had turned it on," Lorry said. "From the moment it started, it acted like it had a driver behind the wheel. Some driver."

"Another inch," I added, "and it would've torn right through the corner of our kitchen."

"Son of a bitch," Peter said, amused. "I'd banish that truck right now. Tell it to go away."

"Look, Peter, don't tell me this thing was a freak accident. What do you make of the emergency brake? It was on the whole time; I heard her pull it."

"Emergency brake must've failed."

"You don't believe in the bizarre, do you, Peter?" Lorry said.

"Bizarre, yes. Supernatural, no. This is bizarre without being the least bit unreal."

"Okay," I said, "let's get scientific. What are the chances of a car starting itself by itself and running into a house?"

"Must be something like a million to one."

He seemed to be enjoying my anger, which was crazy because his vehicle had been ruined.

"Only one million millionth part of an atom is whole," I said. "The rest is empty space."

"Now what is that supposed to mean?" Peter asked.

Nothing bothered him more than irrelevant details thrown into a philosophical or scientific discussion.

"What I'm saying to you is that some things can't be proven or even known, but they're happening to us all the time."

"If you mean that emergency brakes fail, and starter wires short out, and Jeeps will roll when conditions are right, I agree with you."

"Listen. A man snapped a picture of his daughter. She was dressed in her Sunday best when her daddy took the picture. Afterwards in the darkroom, he saw the image of a silver creature standing right behind his own daughter. Some things can't be seen, that's all."

"And . . ." Peter laughed.

"I'm trying to make a point."

"Nothing did in that Jeep but its worn electrical system."

"Maybe you're right."

"All this talk is silly," Lorry said. "I'm just glad I'm not run over like this soup can."

"She's right," I said and gave her a hug.

"Let's pick up all this garbage," Peter said. "I'll get my truck off your house, if you get your wheelbarrow out from under my truck."

27

I knew the time had come to plan an instant getaway, and the best person I could think of to take me up the road to nowhere was my old friend Adam Pereign, who had a cabin up in the mountains north of Santa Fe. I phoned him, and as it turned out, he was planning a fishing trip the next day. He was delighted to have my company. That was all it took to have my bags packed and my hiking boots laced up.

The following day we drove up the road in the early evening, coming to a stop whenever a small creek crossed the road. It was almost summer and the big snows of the past winter were filling the creeks and dry arroyos.

Adam and I found his one-room cabin exactly as he had left it in the fall, with some added mouse droppings and the inescapable evidence of an overnight guest.

"Someone always comes here in the winter and spends a few nights," Adam said. "Probably a hunter. Doesn't bother me. I think it's the same person."

"How do you know?"

"He leaves the place just like he found it, and there's always the same sized lump left in the bed."

While Adam unpacked our things, I took a look around. The cabin—slab-sided pine with the bark on and an overhanging tin roof—was set in a small clearing next to a big hill. Above the hill was a stand of pines and the black trunks left behind by a forest fire, maybe eight or nine years earlier.

Below the cabin a steep incline dropped down to the creek. Directly over the fast-moving water, someone before Adam's time had built a well-framed outhouse. You could sit, flanked by those resinous pines, and read a yellow-paged *Sears Catalogue* from 1936.

The first cold stab of high country air swept down out of the mountains. Adam was making roast beef hash on the Coleman stove by the light of a kerosene lamp when I came back inside.

"Well, how does it feel to get your feet back on the ground?" Adam Pereign was one of my oldest friends. He was a dark, fastidious cabinetmaker who could do most anything he chose. Mainly he was fun to be around because he had a gift for getting as much as possible from every moment.

"It feels good not to have anything to think about," I told him.

"Then have some Wild Turkey."

"That's something I don't have to think about."

We passed the bottle a couple of times before we ate the steaming red hash with scrambled eggs and chili. We also had beer from the cooler, and afterwards, hot coffee. Then more Wild Turkey and a well-packed joint made from some imported grass.

It was good, all of it, especially the silence and the shadow of night coming among the trunks of fir trees. In awhile the field in front of the cabin turned moon-white. The cool air from the creek brought the odor of moss and night things.

I felt warm and well fed. "It's been years since I just got away like this. Not going somewhere on assignment, but just for the hell of it."

"Once I saw a bear come out of that upper clearing," Adam

said. "It stood on its hind feet, paws turned down on its chest, a funny look on its face, sniffing like this . . ." He got up and did his bear-sniffing-dope routine.

"Why not?" I said. "Cats go nuts over catnip. We had one ate so much, it got sick and threw up just like a drunk."

We were passing the bottle of Wild Turkey out on the big unroofed porch, and the sharp taste was good with the grass.

"Want to tell me what happened?" Adam said.

I could hardly see the outline of his face in the dark. Talking to him was like talking to myself in the dark, but better.

"Peter told me some of it," he continued. "He said you'd been into witchcraft."

"I don't know if that describes it. All I know is it's not here now. Let's talk about nature. I'm tired of abnormalities."

"Strange things happen in the high country," he said. "One time I was hiking and I met this guy on a switchback going down toward this little snow-fed lake. He looked kind of strange. Then I saw a kid with him, a boy somewhere around eight or nine. There were scratches and scrapes all over their arms and faces. The kid stood there with his jaw hanging loose and his eyes staring straight ahead.

"I thought that a bear had gotten them, but it turned out they'd been sitting way up on one of those peaks when the mountain under them came loose and started rolling. They jumped and got scratched up, but the rest of their party, a couple of others, was killed. We took a helicopter up where it happened, but we never could dig down deep enough to get them. That was their final resting place."

"That's kind of what happened to me," I said. "Mountain fell on me. Then a truck without a driver tried to run over my wife."

"I heard about that. Pretty unbelievable. Let's go inside. I want to show you something."

The cabin was dark except for the light of the kerosene lamp on the table. Adam brought a white envelope to me. Inside was a small downy feather.

"This is from Second Mesa," he said, preening it gently with his

208

fingertips. "A very close friend, a Hopi, gave it to me. This man died in an epileptic fit, but after he died he returned to our house and stayed for a week. He just walked from room to room. I think he was blessing our house for us. Valerie got scared because Amy was only a baby at the time. Anyway, take this feather. It will bring you good luck; it can protect you against anything."

He took the three-inch bit of fluff, which had come from an eagle's belly, tied a tiny piece of string to it, and returned it to the envelope. He closed the envelope and shook it a few times.

"What was that for?"

"To get corn pollen on it. Without pollen, it won't work." He removed it again and I saw gold-brown specks.

"Put it on that nail over your cot," Adam said.

As I hung my feather guardian on the nail, I realized even Hopi angels couldn't keep my eyes open another minute.

I slept like a drowned man, fully clothed, but woke when I heard a noise in the meadow. My hands holding the wooden spar edges of the cot reminded me who I was. Now where was I and what was making that strange sound?

The rusty high-post bed next to me was empty. A crumpled sleeping bag, thrown open said that someone had left in great haste. My mind clicked on—Adam, the cabin, the empty, moon-filled meadow—and I was awake.

When the noise came again, I recognized it as the snort of a horse. There was another sound like a large fan. I stepped out into the cool night.

Down in the lower meadow, on the other side of the creek, was the outline of a man. Where the big fir trees made a shaggy wall were two horses that I had not seen before. Snorting and stamping, they tossed their manes and moved skittishly in the direction of the forest.

It was a scene from a fairy tale, yet a tension was created by the head-tossing of the horses and the isolated stillness of the figure.

The man was wearing white clothes. Adam had been wearing a white Levi shirt. Of course, it was him. What about the silver pants—was the moonlight turning his faded jeans to sterling?

Then a blue-jeaned man emerged from the shadow of pines that shrouded the outhouse. His arms swayed as he walked—definitely Adam.

The figure in white turned to observe Adam. The silver pants jumped to one side and dropped into a low crouch. A second later, whoever it was made a hard run toward the pines.

Adam was blissfully unaware when he came up to me. I pointed urgently at the north end of the meadow, where a flash of silver shot between the pines and disappeared.

At once, the horses charged frantically into the forest at precisely the same exit the phantom had taken. "What the hell's going on?" Adam said.

"There was a man in white down on the other side of the creek a moment ago. I thought it was you."

"I was taking a crap."

"I know."

"What'd he look like?"

"Tall, very tall. It was too far away to really make out any details. He spooked the moment he saw you coming up the hill."

"Where did those horses come from?"

"They weren't there when we drove up."

"Sometimes there's horses pasturing up here. There's a guy who uses that meadow in the spring and summer, but he's got a whole herd of horses, not just two. Maybe they got separated from the rest."

"I want to have a look," I said, "We should be able to make out tracks with the moon this bright."

We crossed the creek and found the place where the phantom had stood. Tracks showed he had moved about quite a bit before I'd seen him.

The imprints were from ripple-soled boots. They were hard to follow after he made his break for the trees.

In the upper meadow, the hoofprints were deep and moist in the dewy grass. We followed them to the place where they'd broken into the woods. There were broken branches and a strong horse smell.

"Let's go back and get my light," Adam said.

"What for?"

"I don't like trespassers sneaking around in the dark. Let's find who it was and what he was up to."

"I'd rather go back to bed."

"You're the one who's supposed to be an investigative reporter."

"You're forgetting why I'm here in the first place."

We stared at the tunnel in the thick forest, and then Adam shook his head.

"Probably was nothing anyway." He turned to go back toward the creek.

The way he squared his shoulders showed that he was angry with me. He would have stayed that way for awhile if he hadn't been the first one to see the light. A coppery disc appeared over our heads. At first, I thought it was a meteor, but the light flew upward. The orange glow became fluorescent green as it rose, then it shrank to the size of a pinhead and was no longer identifiable.

Adam and I stood in reverent silence.

"I believe we've seen something that'll never be seen again."

"Don't count on it," I said.

"I don't believe I saw that thing."

"Did you hear the sound it made?"

"Like a raven in flight."

"A rushing of air, not a beating sound." It seemed important to get the exact nature of the noise right.

"I don't believe I saw it," he said again. "A UFO—and you saw it with me. We're both sane and not a bit drunk, even if we were a little bit stoned."

Then a loud whinny came from the tunnel in the trees. The sky was going gray now—dawn was near—so we could see maybe fifty feet.

Adam motioned me to follow. I was walking as if my ankles were rubber. Neither one of us talking, we moved through the pines, snapping sharp sticks underfoot. We went steadily uphill to where Adam said the horse tracks dipped off to the right and started going back down in the direction of the creek.

A pine bough knocked off my glasses, and like a complete idiot, I stepped right on them. I could barely see, but all I had to do was concentrate on Adam's white shirt and duck the branches he forgot to hold back for me.

We kept moving along, hunched over. There was a half-inch or more of water in the tracks now; we were very close to the creek.

Then we heard the stamping of soft earth, the occasional hard clang of a horseshoe on a stone. The water was filled with ferns.

"We're near the source," Adam said. "A bit further up, it comes right out of the rocks from underground. This is all snowmelt. Be careful, you could go up to your neck in this stuff."

We were rock-hopping when we saw the first horse already down in the muck, up to its shoulders. It was heaving maniacally to get free, but each thrust took it deeper.

"Get a branch, a log, anything," Adam yelled.

I ran and tripped, falling face down in that slimy backwash. By the time I got to my feet and found a solid log, Adam was struggling to keep the horse's head out of the muck by pulling with all his strength on its halter. He was balancing himself on two rocks while tugging and shouting at the horse—more likely to himself, the big animal had stopped putting up a fight.

"Get that thing under its head," Adam said. "Now if she'll just stay quiet, we can keep her head out of it."

The horse's breathing was constricted; mud was crushed against its ribs. I jammed the log as far as it would go under the head.

"That oughta hold'er." Adam said.

"She's hardly breathing."

"Damn her, she's beginning to like it in there."

"She can't breathe with all the mud on her lungs."

"It's the cold. She's freezing up inside."

For a moment we considered the situation. Adam was covered with mud, his shirt was torn at the shoulder. My clothes were not torn, but I was soaked. Above we could see where the creek sprang out of the earth in pools of ice and streams that laced together into the quagmire where the horse was half breathing.

Now the breathing came harder, more shallow. She gurgled when she exhaled.

"She must've taken water in when she went down the first time," Adam said.

She tried to whinny. A backup gurgle of fetid air and water bubbled out of her nostrils, which opened wide this final time. I let go of the log as the weight became too great and fell backwards into the mud.

Adam lay flat, his right hand braced on a rock, his left glued to the halter.

"Let go, for Christ's sake," I shouted.

He seemed intent on the struggle, and his arm went deeper in the mud. The horse was gone from sight in the dark ooze.

"Adam, let go, you crazy son of a bitch!"

Bracing against a rock, I grabbed his bicep with all my strength. I realized at that moment that his hand was trapped by the halter.

His face was against my right shoulder. I sank my fingers into his bicep and jerked as hard as I could. His hand came free, and taking hold of his shirt collar I began pulling us both back to a dry place.

We lay panting like a couple of hounds. Finally, we got up and, resting on our knees, watched the big oily bubbles where the horse had sunk.

"How's your hand?"

"Not broken, but it hurts like hell."

"Let's go back to the cabin."

It was a good half hour after sunrise.

Adam led the way back to the meadow. The other horse was standing, unmoving, at the other end of the meadow. Its ears were working back and forth.

Slowly, with measured steps, we walked toward it. It kept standing there in that noble pose, ears flicking, flesh rippling from time to time. We came within a few feet, and still the animal stood motionless.

Adam quietly and quickly slipped his unhurt hand under the halter. The horse lowered its head at his touch, and we saw the red-purple sockets where its eyes had been.

Adam was stroking the horse's head. "No wonder it's calm."

"You know, it was so black back there in that swamp and I didn't have my glasses. I couldn't really see the other horse too well."

"Neither one has any eyes."

We led the horse back to the cabin. Neither of us felt like talking. We cleaned off the mud in the creek and attended to the sorrel mare. Her body was unscathed and her face bore no scratch or scrape except the clean, empty eye sockets. If she felt any pain, it had to be minor, since she would permit us to touch around the edge of the eye socket without a shiver.

"What are we going to do with the horse?" I asked.

Adam was biting the bottom of his moustache, looking from the horse to the creek, to the upper end of the meadow. I felt like we had died in that prehistoric muck and come back.

"I can't get my mind off that animal," Adam said.

"This one? She seems alright to me."

"The other one. I keep seeing the way it went down."

"Let me have a look at that hand."

The tissue over the tendons behind the knuckles were rope burned. "Does this hurt here on the bone?"

"It's not broken. Gerry, I know more about injuries than you—my old man was a doctor, remember? So stop worrying about my hand. It's my head that hurts. I got a wicked headache." He was not there at all, and I knew it was up to me to bring him out of that black hole.

"This may kill me," I told Adam, "but I'm going to do it anyway." I headed toward the creek.

"What are you going to do?"

"I'm going to make a sweat bath, like the Indians."

"I'll help," he said, but he just followed me. I made a huge pile of spruce boughs. Then I went back to the cabin for Adam's ax and cut three good-sized pine poles, which I lashed together in a tepee formation. Adam stood there daydreaming, holding his swollen hand in front of him.

214

"What are you making, some kind of shelter?" he asked at last.

"A sweat lodge," I said for the second time. I wove limbs into a bristly tepee. Then I picked up round stones from the creek's edge and made a pile. I put some tinder in the center of the pile and put a match to it. A good flame fanned up right away, and I put on more sticks until I had a nice little blaze. I went up the hill for towels and more of that Wild Turkey.

"What's all this supposed to prove?" he said, still chewing at his mustache.

"Nothing. Something to do until help arrives."

"Are you crazy? No one even knows how to get here. Besides, that fire's dangerous as hell with all this dry pine."

"I don't know what you're going to do for the next fifteen minutes, but I'm going naked into that funny wigwam with those hot rocks. I'm going to drink some more of this firewater, and then I'm going to use the empty bottle to douse the rocks and make them steam, then—"

"You'll freeze your balls off."

"My balls were mutilated a long time ago."

"How are you going to get rocks into that thing without burning yourself, or worse, burning up yourself and my property at the same time?"

"Pick them up with towels."

"You'll burn your hands to a crisp."

"Good. I'll burn my hands."

"Not with my towels you won't."

Adam was being dragged back into the land of the living by his old confidence in his mastery of the irrelevant details of life. He couldn't let a greenhorn get the drop on his superior knowledge of the proper manner of inducing sweat glands to do their thing. He went up to the cabin.

"How about using this?" Adam said with a scowl. He offered me a folding army shovel. It was perfect for scooping up rocks. I made a mound inside the shelter.

"You better take this too," Adam said. He had gone back to the

215

cabin again, this time to fetch me a poncho to cover the opening in front.

"You going to try it?" I asked him.

"Wouldn't dream of it. I'll sit here and watch you make an ass of yourself."

The sun was up, bright and beautiful, but so was the wind. It was too cold for a stunt like this, but it didn't matter. Adam was watching with acute interest now as I killed the bottle of Wild Turkey in two swigs.

"Okay. I'm all set. Here, Adam, fill the bottle for me will you?"

I threw my clothes in a heap. The Wild Turkey helped, but it wasn't a fur coat. I dodged into the little opening scraping my spine on a scratchy limb. I crouched inside like an animal. Adam handed me the bottle of ice cold water, the rocks were smoking and steaming in a pile on the moldy ground, my ass was numb and my feet were, too. I poured the bottle onto the hot rocks just as Adam folded over the poncho and cut out the sunlight.

"How's it feel?"

"Warm as toast," I lied.

The smoke wasn't ventilating. Not only was I freezing at the back and burning at the front, where the rocks were giving off steam heat, but I was not breathing anything but pine-clogged smoke. All this to get Adam out of his funk. He looked in and saw me huddled, in the gloom, arms wrapped about my knees, teeth chattering. He was stomping and howling out there, and I was contemplating a pounce to the throat and a ritual tearing of enemy flesh. Instead I got out of the sweat lodge, scraping my spine in the same place with the same feverishly sharp branch, and danced into some of my clothes, paying no attention to which was underwear and which was pants or shirt. I made it back to the cabin and did the whole mess over again. He was there making some coffee. A fire was roaring in the stove.

"If you only could have seen that crouched animal-look you had in that thing."

He was moving around with his old confidence. He was back to being the man who can do everything, the master of the moment.

"Adam," I said after a few mouthfuls of scalding coffee, "what do you want to do now?"

"I want to see you stuck in the back of that sweat lodge with your face all covered with pitch and smoke, trying to breathe, with your chin on your knees. That was the funniest goddamned thing I ever . . ."

"Adam, I am asking a serious question. What do you want to do next? Do you think we ought to report this thing? If so, we'd better head back to the Tesuque Ranger Station."

"Who says we have to do anything? You said yourself the horse is alright. Its owner is up here every couple of days. We'll leave it tied up by the cabin so it won't run off and get hurt."

"I'm not worried about the horse. I'm thinking of us."

"You mean you're afraid we have implicated ourselves just by having seen what we've seen?"

"That's exactly what I mean. This is the first mute I have ever been this close to. I'm not saying I'm afraid."

"Yes, you are, and you'd be a fool if you weren't. I'm scared shitless myself. I'm thinking seriously of selling the place and never coming back."

"That's up to you and Valerie."

"I'm going to do it, I tell you. I want never to see this shithole again."

"Adam, listen to me. We have to have some kind of plan."

"Hey, are you trying to tell me that you're going to write this thing up in the *Review*?"

"Partly. It's my job."

"Job my ass. You think I'll be able to sell the place if you write all this mess up in the papers? It'll be on national news in no time."

"I know that. What I want to know is whether you'd be willing to testify that the light we saw was a UFO."

"I'm going to shut my mouth and never breathe a word of this thing as long as I live. If you write about it, that's your business, but you'd better leave me and this place out of it, because I'll deny anything you put in the paper. If I ever do forget what happened up in that bog, it'll be a miracle. Do you want some breakfast? I'm going to heat up some of last night's hash with eggs."

"That sounds real good. Tell me this, and then I'll shut up. Do you think trouble is following me? Do you think this was brought on by me and my job?"

"If I were you, Gerry, I'd tell Atkins to cram it, and I'd get the hell out of investigative writing. It isn't much fun to be threatened the way you have been the past three months. Man, you've stuck your neck out. In my opinion, you've done your job too well. Now back off. Didn't you tell me there were signs once before?"

"There've been plenty of signs. White dogs taking blood baths. A travel van in the middle of an arroyo in the middle of nowhere, spooky telephone calls, spookier friends, evil thoughts that clutch your brain, invisible snakes, runaway vehicles—not to mention visitors from outer space. Okay, so you won't talk about it. I ought to bottle it up, too, and let this be the end."

He began serving up the hash. Now I was the one in need of help.

"I think you're crazy to sell this place."

"We were on the verge of selling it anyway. We need the money. Besides, unlike you, I believe in signs. What happened today is a sign saying get the hell out while you're still able."

We packed up slowly and methodically, each of us making private resolutions. My life was a mess. It had started back the night with Hannah when I saw the dog, and it had begun to get out of hand when I first met Etienne. Why did I allow myself to trust him? Wasn't he dangerously insane? Lorry had warned me about him time after time. Why had I allowed myself to get sucked into this situation? Poor Adam selling his land. I was feeling guilty as hell.

Etienne, Harjac, that guy in the arroyo, Dr. Fell, old Kreuger—the hunters of evil seemed as wicked as the evildoers themselves. Gomez was a trigger-happy little kid. Maybe his job was to throw everyone off the trail. Hell, anything was possible. I had truly seen the varmint. Well, that was what Atkins had wanted—that

218

ambassador of goodness. His perfect timing and eternal confidence made me sick.

"What are you doing? The car's all packed and ready to go, and you're just sitting there clenching your fists. Gerry, let's get out of here, now." He was a good old Adam again, someone who had better things to do than wreak revenge on things inside his head.

"Don't forget this." He held up my feather. "It'll still protect, if you let it." It was meaningless to me, but I couldn't tell him that now.

For the first few miles, we rumbled down the road in silence. We retraced the same bends in the road and pitched over the same junctures of creek and sandbed.

The roads below were drier, the meadows greener. We both wanted to concentrate on the scenery, but there was nothing to see but empty road and the whip of willows against our tires along the last few miles of the Tesuque Fire Road back to civilization.

As we rounded the last elbow turn, Adam eased off the accelerator. The van came slowly to a stop.

"Will you look at that? I've been by here a thousand times, and this is the first time I ever saw anything like that. That's pueblo grazing land."

Scattered today on the hillside weren't cattle, but twenty or thirty shaggy elk.

"Will you look at that?" Adam said. "I've been by here a hundred thousand times in my life, and this is the first time I ever saw anything like that."

They were mostly cows, dark brown stilt-legged animals, down from their winter range. They looked skinny.

"Must have been a hard winter," I said.

"They live off the burns in the upper ranges; the new growth comes up real plentiful. I guess it must be all gone by now. I've never seen them down this low before, and in cattle country."

The scene of all these contented animals should have calmed my nerves, but it didn't. All I could think of was an interview I had read about one of the few mutilations of wild animals. A hunter up in Montana somewhere who claimed to have shot an elk with a 30-30, then watched as his elk got sucked up into the sky by some invisible force. The hunter later found the elk mutilated in the classic contemporary mode.

"Look how the bulls keep watch," Adam said. "They keep their heads up all the time the cows eat."

"I wonder why they're not scared of us."

"They know when it's elk season and when it isn't."

The van began to roll again. The elk held their positions resolutely, some of them watching us as we drove off. I was reminded again of driving away from the pueblo being watched by the wall of untelling eyes of a whole herd of cattle.

After five or ten miles of canyon country, we came out in scrub oak and pine foothills. Now we could see the Tesuque Valley and the valleys beyond, and the mesas of the distant pueblos. Blue dusk rolled in and faraway things turned to haze. Time hung very still.

The warm air from the dusty highway going down into the lowlands blew into my face. Looking at the limitless hills, I felt like I had felt the first time I went for a long run at seven thousand feet. My heart had wanted to burst from the strain, but as long as there was a trail in front of me and nothing to stop my feet, there was no stopping my mind—and it was my mind that was doing the running. My mind was doing the running now, too. I didn't have to be a prisoner of circumstances: I had a future. Then I realized how easy it would be to break away.

I had an overriding desire to burn all of my old notes. J.R.'s father had said if he had only burned the sheep skins that day, he would have saved his sheep and kept his family safe. I was going to get back into that file and destroy every last note.

Adam let me out in front of the *Review*.

"You're okay now?"

"Yeah, I'm fine. Still a little shook up, but I'll be alright after I get finished here."

"Take care, and remember, you've got a job waiting at my shop.

220

You'd make a damn fine cabinetmaker."

He drove off into the sunset. I had seen too many suns going down these last months, and too many moons coming up. I wanted to work with my hands for a change, and Adam's offer sounded too good to be true.

I listened for footsteps in the outer office. There was the silence of a dead Sunday office; all the ghosts had gone home to watch television. I pictured Jamie Atkins getting into his third Sunday suit of the day for an evening of public speaking.

I looked at Jamie's desk: the exquisite order, the magnificence of the open date book, the call-back notes on their nail hook, the integrated stacks of manuscripts, the great black logbook where he kept the company secrets.

"I quit," I said to the empty room.

I found the file folders in the bottom of my second drawer. I took them out back to the incinerator used by the restaurant that adjoined our building, and gave them the deep six. In the entrance of the restaurant was a phone. As I dialed our number, I noticed that people were watching me. Then I remembered the charcoal on my face. I had never completely cleaned up after my cataclysmic sweat bath.

"You're safe," Lorry said. "Thank God."

My voice sounded calm in the chamber of the phone. Well, I was beginning to feel calm after all these mad months.

"I'll be right there. Don't move an inch."

"I'm quitting the *Review*."

"I know. Adam already told me. I can't wait to see you. I'll be right there. Don't move an inch."

People were staring at me, but I didn't care. I was going home. I sat down at the counter and ordered a cup of coffee.

It must be twilight now in the grazing meadow. I saw the last elk move away from the meadow. There was nothing on the grass except ghost hoofprints. The elk were free to move about the forest as they pleased. Now night was on the meadow, starlight on the grass. Nothing interfered with space and time but the veils of light and dark. The meadow required no understanding.

ABOUT THE AUTHOR

GERALD A. HAUSMAN has been a magazine editor, book publisher, poet-in-residence, and newspaper reporter since his graduation from New Mexico Highlands University in 1968. He has been a member of the staff of the Sunstone Press, a distinguished publisher of southwestern books and notecards, and has recently been appointed vice president. Hausman is the author of several nonfiction books, including *Sitting on the Blue-eyed Bear: Navajo Myths and Legends* and *The Night Herding Song*.